Shadow Craft

Shadow Craft

Visual Aesthetics of Black and White Hindi Cinema

Gayathri Prabhu
Nikhil Govind

BLOOMSBURY
NEW DELHI • LONDON • OXFORD • NEW YORK • SYDNEY

BLOOMSBURY INDIA
Bloomsbury Publishing India Pvt. Ltd
Second Floor, LSC Building No. 4, DDA Complex, Pocket C – 6 & 7,
Vasant Kunj, New Delhi 110070

BLOOMSBURY, BLOOMSBURY ACADEMIC INDIA and the Diana logo are trademarks of Bloomsbury Publishing Plc

First published in India 2021
This edition published 2021
This paperback edition published 2025

Bloomsbury Academic
An imprint of Bloomsbury Publishing Plc

ISBN: PB: 978-93-69521-94-4; eBook: 978-93-90176-26-7

2 4 6 8 10 9 7 5 3 1

Typeset in Minion Pro by Manipal Technologies Limited
Printed and bound in India

Contents

Note on Images and Translation

The following is the format for image citation: When a frame is discussed in a standalone manner, it is designated as Fig. 1, Fig. 2, Fig. 3, etc.; when discussed as separate shots of a continuous sequence, it is designated as Fig. 1.1, Fig. 1.2, or Fig. 2.1, Fig. 2.2, etc.; when discussed as separate frames within the same shot, it is designated as Fig. 1A, Fig. 1B, etc.

All images in this book (except one) are credited with much gratitude to the National Film Archive of India, Pune.

All translations from the film (dialogue, voice-over) are by the authors. The first time the title of a film is mentioned (in the Introduction and the relevant chapter), its English translation is given. After this, the film will be referred by the Hindi title.

In Gratitude

We wholeheartedly acknowledge our gratitude to the National Film Archive of India (NFAI)—the images in this book would not have been possible without the generous permission of its Director, Prakash Magdum. If we needed any insight on how individuals buoy institutions, then we had to look no further than Reema Murthi, Rahul A. and Amit Patil at NFAI—their warm support and effort came when it was most needed.

This manuscript has been incubated entirely within the beautiful campus-town of Manipal in Karnataka, more specifically at the Manipal Centre for Humanities. Many of these ideas were discussed in classrooms with our students, and the company of young cinema enthusiasts fed our spirits. We fussed about each image we wanted to share with the readers, timing it to the micro-second, and this would not have been possible without the patient research assistance provided by Yadukrishnan P.T. who represents a promising generation of film scholarship. It was equally a comfort to draw from the artistic finesse of Mariam Henna and Nikhil Ravishankar, as well as the logistical competency of Urmila G. A conversation about song and lyric with Simona Sawhney became an anchoring moment. Asha Shivanand saw the possibilities in our partnership from the start and sustained us with her positive outlook. Kailashnath Koppikar's experience and knowledge of film production in Mumbai have been an incubator for many ideas explored over the years. As we revised the manuscript, Srijan Deshpande nourished our personal education in appreciating soundscapes and offered crucial details. Shaurya Rahul Narlanka patiently addressed ongoing queries on technology and persuaded us to acquire the device that successfully captured the cinematic frames at the archive. We were fortunate to have next-door-office inputs of film scholar Mohamed Shafeeq Karinkurayil and the experience of a national workshop that he organised with Ashish Rajadhyakshya. Other scholars of Indian cinema that we had an opportunity to engage with in Manipal include Madhava Prasad, S.V. Srinivas and Ratheesh Radhakrishnan. T.M. Krishna composed sections of *Sebastian & Songs* during a brief residency at our Centre, a cherished camaraderie of parallel writing (his book on sound, this book on image) late into rain-lashed monsoon evenings. The encouragement of colleagues at the Manipal Centre for Humanities and the Student Support Centre, Manipal, was vital during long bouts of withdrawal and writing. We are deeply thankful to this circle of kindness and magnanimity.

It is a privilege to work with an editor who stays with the pulse of the writer and supports the process of an idea becoming a book with perfect synchronicity. Chandra Sekhar of Bloomsbury has our gratitude for this. We were helped in our efforts to collate the required images and formulate a visual language for this book by Arvind Booni. We are thankful to Shreya Chakraborti and the team at Bloomsbury for their care with the manuscript.

We owe much to Arush Kishore for his attentiveness, calm counsel and the pleasure of knowing Tvisha. We have benefitted from decades of vitality and nurturance from Sanghamitra Misra and Rahul Govind. Chirayu Patel's wide-ranging and keen interests have fortified us, as also the joyous times with Arushi and Advay.

The longest companion to Gayathri's exploration of aesthetics has been her sister Greeshma. An eager childhood accomplice to film viewings, a gifted visual artist and intuitive ally for any form or light that speaks beauty, Greeshma's unfailing love and strength is embedded deep in this work.

For their lifelong enthusiasm towards vintage films, we remain indebted to our parents: Geetha Prabhu, Raji Govind and I.K. Govind. Their continued passion for older melodies and artists has added much pleasure to our writing process. We dedicate this book to them.

Introduction: The Promise of Black and White Cinema in Independent India

The Establishing Shot

A young woman, unfamiliar with the city or its cinematic culture, has come to a film studio to return a coat that had been lent to her during a rainstorm. She is holding the coat and a card she found in the coat—on it is the name of a film director. The young woman steps through the studio doorway straight into the film set and is walking a deserted alleyway with lit windows. Silence. She is suddenly aware of nearly stepping on the only other person in that space, a man propped against a column (perhaps drunk, perhaps a beggar) who mutters something. She flinches, jumps back and her steps quicken. She has not noticed the dark wheels of a camera crane move stealthily towards her, but the viewer does, and we track across the frame to spy on this meeting of woman and camera. Her face, not far from us, turns up sharply. Her eyes dart in panic and she starts to move backwards. Coming towards her is the machine—a camera and its lens mounted on a crane, held by strangers. The camera glides straight ahead, unrelenting. Her face continues to retreat, eyes flickering like a caged animal, till her head rests against her own shadow on the wall. Cut, cut, cut! A cacophony of voices burst out. Who is this, and how did she walk into the middle of a shot being filmed? She explains—she has come to return a coat to the film's director, the one sitting on the crane, his arm confidently stretched beside the camera (Fig. 1.1 to Fig. 1.5). Having offered her explanation, the woman walks ahead into the shadows of the studio and the camera continues to do its work.

Fig. 1.1 *Source NFAI*

Fig. 1.2 *Source NFAI*

Fig. 1.3 *Source NFAI*

Fig. 1.4 *Source NFAI*

Fig. 1.5 *Source NFAI*

This scene in Guru Dutt's *Kaagaz ke Phool* (Flowers of Paper, 1959) comes about twenty-eight minutes into the over-two-hour-long film. The metafiction of the script has been obvious to the viewers from its opening shot—a film about the making and unmaking of films as seen through its central protagonist, a director who has known cinematic success in his youth and destitution in his old age. However, this metafiction—the loving exploration of studio spaces, gliding vistas up and down the lighting scaffold, the buzz of a crew at work, conversations about the angst of making cinema—is yet to impact the viewer's consciousness as it does in the third shot of the sequence described earlier (Fig. 1.3). This specific shot, after the young woman walks into the film set, after she looks up in alarm, is her point of view—a close frontal shot of the lens of the camera that is filming her. Even though this is the woman's perspective, it is primarily an encounter of two cameras—one is a moving charged prop and the second camera is doing the actual filming as it emotes her fear. The prop camera, helmed by the director that is within the frame and supposed to be filming is in reality blind—whereas the woman's point of view, supposed to be the captured and reactive image, is in truth the active image and meaning-making filmic vehicle. In this tight dark frame, where the large, black, looming camera descends towards the viewer, the viewer suddenly finds herself thrown into the frame, standing in for the second camera, defiantly returning the gaze. It is a moment of joyous self-recognition—the industry acknowledging its own craftsmanship, its moment of birth, promise and possibility.[1]

The present study locates itself in the returned gaze of this encounter between two camera-selves and it does so in the light–shade visual aesthetics of post-independence cinema in Hindi. The black and white cinema from the late 1940s to the early 1960s has been acknowledged as formative, especially in terms of thematic questions of a new Nehruvian citizenship. However, the present project is less focused on thematics alone and is more invested in the intersection of this thematic with a self-conscious and self-fashioning visual aesthetic that is concerned with the very construction of that thematic. The cinematic output of this period shows explicit concern with the process of film-making as much as the images that result and regulate the theme. These films explored themes in a richness, variety and boldness that has rarely been matched—and this exploration of themes has been correlated with equivalent confidence in the appropriation and creation of an apposite, precisely imagined visual language that scholarship has not yet adequately appreciated. The filming in black and white allowed film-makers an unprecedented array of exploration of pools of dark and shadow, of habitation, of texture and of location (studio and the nascent explorations of the outdoor). The sumptuous visual language gets mapped onto affective registers—for instance, the angst of the artist (*Aag* and *Pyaasa*), the loneliness of the neglected wife (*Sahib Bibi aur Ghulam*), the claustrophobia of the woman prisoner (*Bandini*), the romance of haunted selves and architectures (*Mahal*). Oriented towards these registers, this book is anchored mainly around five directors—Kamal Amrohi, Raj Kapoor, Bimal Roy, Guru Dutt and Abrar Alvi—and the earliest of the films that we study (*Aag*) was released in 1948, while the last in chronology is *Bandini* in 1963. The overlapping and bracketing of these dates with Nehru's term as the first Prime Minister of independent India (1947–1964) becomes more than a coincidence and underlines the porous sociopolitical milieu that fashioned and impacted the aesthetics of the time.

For now, we return to the studio floor. The terse conversation between the director sitting beside the camera on the crane and the woman-intruder with the coat who is pinned against the wall—as much by the studio lights as by the collective gaze of crew and camera—ends with his suggestion that she sit down while he takes his shot ('*Main shot le loon, phir aap se baat karta hoon*'). During this conversation that includes a view from over the woman's shoulder, the camera mounted on the crane is again featured prominently (similar to Fig. 1.5)—it sits at the centre of the frame in a halo of light, ponderous, its lens resolutely looking down at us. Neither the preoccupied director nor the trespassing woman has registered that the camera has already filmed her and that the 'wrong' footage is effectively a screen test—the director later sees the rushes and decides to make her the heroine of the film.

As the woman walks out of the frame to take her seat, the shot is reminiscent of the earlier establishing shot of her walking through the film set. In this visual resolution, the giant apparatus of the crane and its wheels are silhouetted in the foreground even as several bent backs and skilled hands pull it back. The trespassing woman, also silhouetted, walks towards us as our vision tracks backwards—the filming camera (the viewer) is now entirely synchronous (in motion and perspective) with the mounted prop of the active camera. Deep in the lit part of the frame, a young man runs in with a clapperboard. The show is about to begin.

Scripting the Storyboard

On 7 July 1896, the first film screening was held in India—six short titles by the Lumiere Brothers for an admission fee of one rupee—and the venue was the 'whites-only' Watson's Hotel in Bombay.[2] It took seventeen years from that screening at the Watson's to the production of the first film by an Indian director—*Raja Harishchandra* (King Harishchandra, 1913) by D.G. Phalke—and the production was hailed as a 'swadeshi moving picture' in Lokamanya Tilak's weekly *Kesari*,[3] as being Indian even before it was quite acknowledged as being cinema. An advertisement for the film (dated 28 June 1913) invited patrons to a screening of *Raja Harishchandra* at Alexandra Theatre, calling it 'An Entirely Indian Production by Indians' and featured one word that was repeated in prominent font size—'SEE'.[4] Four displays were listed beside this invitation to a visual feast—the royal tiger hunt, the fire in the jungle, the burning ghats of Benaras and the apparition of Mahadev. In smaller font, just below this was the assurance of a 'usual abundance of comics'. While the pride in the indigenous production was being evoked, the identity of this new production and format was also trying to define itself by content and spectacle—as a visual feast and a wholesome fare of drama, mythology and comedy. Unwittingly, this advertisement became a prescient profile of the mixed-genre quality of mainstream cinema in the country.

By the time Phalke (1870–1944) made his 1917 film *Lanka Dahan* (Lanka Aflame!), which featured episodes from the Hindu epic Ramayana, it was clear that the audience was fixated on the medium and that the medium was capable of huge profits.[5] Whether for love of the medium or the money, the logistics of film-making and the need to create new screening spaces would invariably recreate something of the studio culture of the American film industry in Bombay, especially with the figure of J.F. Madan (and later the Wadia brothers) who financed several film projects and built screening halls. During a visit to New York, Madan watched Warner Brothers' *The Jazz Singer* (1927), the first feature-length film with synchronised dialogue. He came back to India determined to introduce the possibility of sound to Indian cinema and its viewers, but a reversal of his business fortunes meant the Indian film industry had to continue making silent films till 1931 when Ardeshir Irani directed *Alam Ara* (The Ornament of the World). This meeting of visual and sound remains mostly for the records, as no known copy of the film has been available since 1967.[6]

Nonetheless, this moment of sound and visual coming together on celluloid becomes a precursor to the films of the 1940s, with its full embrace of song and drama, of dialogue and theatrical performance.

Through these decades, as the fledgling industry consolidated its craft and technology, it continued to lure its audience again and again to the cinema halls. It is important to note that this is happening against the daily lived realities of the two world wars, a time of economic scarcity and black-marketing and an accelerating nationalist movement. Soon enough, we have the regeneration and rupture that 1947 came to represent, not only in terms of colonial rule and new nationhood but in the reverberations of Partition in the film industry itself. Several artists—such as music director Ghulam Haider, singer Noor Jehan, writer Sadat Hasan Manto—migrated to the new state of Pakistan, disrupting deep creative and commercial partnerships. In a real-life filmy tale of thwarted brotherhood, actor Nasir Khan moved to Lahore for a few years while his brother Yusuf Khan (Dilip Kumar) stayed back in Bombay as his fortunes as the leading man and indeed his reputation as the 'king of tragedy' continued to rise. The city of Bombay and its film industry had to make room for refugees who had trekked from across the border in search of livelihood and survival. Irrespective of which direction the migration went, the scars of religious differentiation and devastation were all too immediate and painful. It would not be far-fetched to suggest that both the bleakness of loss and the celebration of new identity came to be sutured until they could not be easily told apart.

Scholars have commented on the ambivalences that people both within and outside the industry felt towards commercial cinema at this time. Sumita S. Chakravarty writes of the unstable financial situation following the war, when 'several films failed at the box office and a general climate of fault-finding and criticism was prevalent'.[7] Several veterans of the industry could not 'reconcile themselves to the film industry's emphasis on formula, stars, extravagance and freelancing for the sake of "entertainment"'.[8] Consequently, according to

Ravi Vasudevan, as the dust of Partition slowly settled and a new decade rolled out, the dominant critical discussion of commercial cinema was largely negative—the industry was censured for

> a tendency to *stasis* at the level of narrative and character development; an emphasis on externality, whether of action or character representation; melodramatic (florid, excessive) sentimentality; crude or naïve plot mechanisms such as coincidence; narrative dispersion through arbitrary performance sequences; and unrestrained and over-emotive acting styles.[9]

This perception was likely a result of the emerging and bifurcated creative territories between commercial and parallel or art cinema (the celebrated Bengali film *Pather Panchali* was released in 1955 and its director Satyajit Ray was among those who wrote about these aesthetic divergences). However, as has been extensively studied and commented regarding the upsurge of musicals in Hollywood in the aftermath of the Great Depression in America, one can perhaps sense a similar reimagining in the mainstream cinema community, and it often emerged through active participation with other artistic forums—Raj Kapoor in Prithvi Theatre, Guru Dutt in Uday Shankar's dance troupe, Chetan Anand in the Indian People's Theatre Association. Hollywood was also a significant source of inspiration—Ravi Vasudevan points out its imprint in the point of view techniques and continuity editing adopted by Indian directors in the 1950s, even as these films 'displayed an investment in the burden of melodramatic subjection as it was relayed through characters caught in the vortex of social marginality and indignity'.[10] The technical innovations were oriented towards the transnational, and the modernist and the thematic explorations also sought to represent the universal ethical compass of a collective conscience. For instance, Guru Dutt's *Kaagaz ke Phool* evokes Orson Welles's *Citizen Kane* (1941) during several cinematic moments though the 'rich man' in the Hindi film is fated to slip to abject poverty and destitution before any psychological longing can be (un)resolved.

It remains fairly indisputable that while various states/languages in India established their respective studio cultures and cinematic genealogies during these crucial years, the genesis and development of a shared cinematic culture in India kept the city of Bombay as its fulcrum. Here, we are in sympathy with Rosie Thomas's rationale for the usage of 'Bombay' instead of 'Mumbai'—the former standing in for a secular, multifaith city that was renamed in 1995.[11] The focus on the city helps us understand why the Hindi film industry—before the word 'Bollywood' was coined by film journalism in the 1970s—dominated popular imagination and became synonymous for mainstream Indian cinema despite the blind spots of the 'Hindi-Hindu-Hindustan' slogan that was in circulation through the 1930s and 1940s. Priya Joshi reads the word 'Bollywood' as a historical marker that underscores the prominent role of the 1970s in constituting modern India—as conveying 'a cinema in which popular and mass, politics and pleasure are inextricably linked and are discernible far beyond, and even before, the moment of naming'.[12] Ashish Rajadhyaksha has suggested that the word refers not only to Hindi cinema but encompasses a larger culture industry of which cinema is only one part.[13] Ravi Vasudevan responded to this by making it historically specific to the release of *Dilwale Dulhaniya Le Jayenge* (The Brave-hearted Will Take the Bride, 1995) with its growing 'transnational aesthetic impulses and multiple sites of reception' that are largely oriented to the global nation and for foreign, cross-over audiences.[14] Irrespective of whether we agree on a definition, the coinage and usage of the word 'Bollywood' has been reclaimed as a positive identity by several scholars and practitioners and can be read as an indicator of the shift in the aesthetics of the industry itself—perhaps even invite us to see the 1970s as the initial break, the start of a new self-conscious aesthetics that becomes Bollywood. That conjecture is outside the purview of our study but it helps us think about why our interest in the black and white visual aesthetics stays within the time frame of the late 1940s to the mid-1960s. Unlike a study of silent cinema, where there is a clear chronology of films before and after sound (despite some lag and overlaps), there is no similar etched demarcation between black and white and colour. Colour film came on Indian screens as early as *Kisan Kanya* (The Peasant Girl, 1937) and moved fully into the realm of technological and financial sustainability in 1952 with Mehboob Khan's *Aan* (Honour, starring Dilip Kumar and Nimmi). *Aan* was followed by celebrated films, such as *Jhanak Jhanak Payal Baaje* (The Sound of Anklets by V. Shantaram in 1955) and Mehboob Khan's *Mother India* in 1957. Yet, black and white film-making lingered even as colour became popular and it is this lingering that offers us space to think about shifting visual aesthetics, even as the Bombay film industry prepared for the coming of new technologies and even as the nation prepared for the inevitable end of Nehru's premiership. Someswar Bhowmik in *Censorship in Cinema* points out that the cinema of the 1950s 'textually constructed the core of the spectator by laying before him/her two crucial axes of melodrama and spectacle on the silver screen'.[15] One might even argue that the films made in black and white during this period, whether by choice or financial considerations, were acutely aware of the inevitability of change and these last flares of nostalgia embraced the black-white-grey scale with renewed eyes and passion, eager to push it to its full expression. This would also be the last generation that would 'not' see black and white visuality as an absence of colour but as an assertive elaborate palette of textures, of intricate filigrees of dappled light, of deep tones of shadows, a complex vehicle to capture human interiorities and frailties at their nuanced best.

More than any other art form in India, the gap between the creative output and the critical apparatus is quite stark with cinema. As Neepa Majumdar reminds us, 'cinema's status as guilty pleasure in India was mirrored not only in its relative absence from mainstream intellectual discourse but also in its absence as a respectable field of study'.[16] For a country that produces the largest number of films in the world, books on cinema are sparse in comparison. Many books do begin with a conversation about the need to produce more scholarship but there is also a strong awareness of how the sparseness of field has necessitated and even facilitated a broad array of academic approaches. By casting its net wide, in terms of theme and modalities, scholarship has thrown up some patterns that are worth revisiting and taking into consideration before any new approach is discussed. The discursive entry points in tracking Hindi cinema of the twentieth century are diverse. As the film historian Lalit Joshi comments on the broader mid-century Hindi public sphere, 'Indian cinema—its narrativity, cinematography, dramaturgy, aesthetics, morality, and social relevance—became the foci of intense literary contemplation.'[17] Rosie Thomas gravitates to specific genres like action and fantasy films (from the 1930s to the 1960s) combined with ethnographic fieldwork in the Bombay film industry (during the 1980s) to explore cultural hybridity.[18] For Madhava Prasad, who undertakes the daunting task of offering a theoretical framework for the field, this possibility lies in 'the emergence of the modern state as a sole supervising authority over the [nuclear] family'—the family is depicted on screen as the site of this tension.[19] Ravi Vasudevan examines 'melodrama as a mode, modality and genre in specific historical, political and film industrial contexts'.[20] For Anil Saari, the study of cinema takes into account social articulation of collective dreams, an agential space of liberation from the dogmatic, idealistic world of morality and religion.[21] Someswar Bhowmik studies censorship laws and practices in post-independent India as separate from its colonial origins and embedded in the contemporary propagation of a political agenda. Sumita S. Chakravarty shapes her study around the genre of stunt films that disappeared during 'the nation-building decade' of the 1950s as well as the role of the writer in cinema. Neepa Majumdar studies female stardom in which equivalences were made between cinema, stardom, femininity and nation.[22] M.K. Raghavendra locates his interest in the manner in which Indian cinema narrativises social experience to examine the system according to which its codes have been employed, largely in relation to Hollywood.[23] Nasreen Munni Kabir works through the mode of the biography by focusing on one cinematic figure (director, producer and actor Guru Dutt) to reflect on the larger sociocultural matrix that shaped and sustained this figure.[24] Rachel Dwyer examines the relationship between film and religion as a way of examining the religious imagination in India as it has been manifested in the film as a major form of public culture.[25] Ruth Vanita writes of the figure of the courtesan in Hindi cinema speaking in the ambiguous voice of the modern nation, inviting spectators to seek both pleasure and the meaning of life.[26] Editors Sangita Gopal and Sujata Moorti in their 'Introduction' to a collection of essays focus on Bollywood song and dance as providing 'a repertoire of images, visualities and performance idioms that articulate with local concerns at different reception sites'.[27] One of the few monographs that explicitly focus on the visual culture of Hindi cinema is a collaborative effort between Rachel Dwyer and Divia Patel: while Patel approaches this visuality through a study of advertising and promotional material, Dwyer offers an understanding of visual culture as all that contributes to the 'look' of a film—sets, locations and fashion (costumes, makeup, etc.). It is significant that the 'look' here is about the given components within the frame rather than the considerations (lens, camera-movements and lights) that went into the making of that frame.[28]

The previous sampling of the scholarship thus suggests three clustering—the films are read either thematically or historically/contextually or through audience reception/spectatorship. But for a few moments of close reading of the compositional elements in specific scenes, shots and frames, the scholars tend to privilege reading of the film through reception and plot (storyline, characterisation, dialogue, song). The challenge of leading with the thematic or historical or spectatorship models is that it sidelines the question of aesthetics—in other words, the visual and performative choices involved in synthesising sound, light and composition in the construction of the theme tends to get downplayed in the quest for overarching post-facto meaning. In contradistinction, this project is an attempt to explore aesthetics by looking at a key unit of the composition of the film—the cinematic frame—and more specifically the relationship of that visual with the black and white palette that represented (roughly) first fifteen formative years of post-independence Indian cinema.

The Preview

As with the genesis of most new technologies, there is no sharp break or demarcation point between the production of black and white films and films made in colour—nor did the possibilities of capturing colour in celluloid make obsolete the aesthetics of black and white. Through the 1950s, Technicolor films continued to be made alongside black and white—the 1960s saw the advent of Eastman colour with *Hum Hindustani* (We Indians, 1961) and *Junglee* (Wild, 1961). The earliest production discussed in this book, *Aag* (Fire, 1948), and the most recent *Bandini* (Female Prisoner, 1963) are contemporaries of films exploring colour. However, by the start of the 1970s, the acceptance of colour was an irreversible norm.

The attitude towards black and white cinema after the advent of colour, Richard Misek reminds us (in the global context), has largely been 'perceived in one of two ways: in its presence prior to the mid-1960s as an aesthetic default, and in its presence since the mid-1960s as an occasional idiosyncrasy'.[29] The 'aesthetic default' has been studied by film scholars for the range of visual expressions made possible by the material quality of the black and white medium. *The Encyclopedia of Hindi Cinema* dwells on how the invariable reproduction of colours as shades of grey made the black and white cinematographer's art one of 'creating a tonal separation between these different shades of grey'—this could only be done by lighting and the right choice of lens.[30] In the subsequent transition from black and white film to colour cinema, it is inevitable that several distinct visual expressions (formed or contributed by the materiality of the film) would itself be phased out. This book's premise, however, is that the black and white aesthetic, far from being the absence of colour or merely a technological fact (only silver nitrate film was available at that historical moment), was instead, through the effort of several talented directors, actors, lyricists, technicians and so on, a fully fleshed and realised aesthetic. This book offers multiple instances of these bold forays in the use of light, designing a frame, choreographing action, pacing and editing—it is thus vital that these visual elements be used to read the films on their own terms, whatever the explicit plot and genre thematics of the film may have been. The most singular accomplishment of this era was perhaps the triumph of the expressive shadow—hence the title of this book. *Shadow Craft* is the evocativeness of several images made possible by these contrasts of lighting—what the greyscale enabled was a specific exploration of shadow on screen, an image-set that may be said to define the labour of a whole generation of aesthetics. Further, like the relation of light and shadow, the understanding of space is also a basic building block to the aesthetic of the studio era—the historical studio lot of the 1940s allowed for the creation of particularised and controlled formal spaces within the film—it has already been shown how the site of production is directly thematised in *Kaagaz ke Phool*. This investment in form and architecture makes a fortuitous opening for this book with one of the earliest films in this selection: Kamal Amrohi's *Mahal* (Mansion, 1949). The *mahal* or palace/mansion in which wandering desires are trapped is a powerful metaphor for the walls, ceilings, doors, windows and landscapes that spatialise/open-up cinema. The visual encoding of the opulent phantasmal *mahal* puts in place a distinct and influential idiom of visual language—this forms an Overture (and thus the first chapter) to the study.

The fixity of the mortar and brick legacy of *Mahal* fragments into the tempestuous elements of fire, water and air with *Aag* (Fire, 1948), *Barsaat* (Rain, 1949) and *Aah* (The Sigh, 1953) in Raj Kapoor's cinema. One might even see the earth element in *Shree 420* (The Gentleman Cheat, 1955) where the Chaplinesque opening scene of a tramp at a crossroad dwells on dust being shaken out of his disintegrating shoes. While scholars have written on the resonating influences of Raj Kapoor's onscreen persona in *Andaz* (Style, 1949), *Awaara* (The Vagabond, 1951) and *Shree 420*, and the canonical nature of these films in how they form a commentary on Nehruvian socialism and nation-building, not enough has been said about the effervescent passion that Raj Kapoor sought to create in his earlier and more formative films like *Aag* and *Barsaat*. One might even argue that one can trace the origins and achievement of Kapoor's cinematic style (the composition of scenes, the play of indoors–outdoors, notions of 'staging' versus spontaneity and the emotive churn of natural elements) to these early directorial offerings. This is the second chapter.

Two contentious questions have vexed our discussions—the first is the assumption that the visual aesthetics of a film can be sourced predominantly to its director and the second is the niggling sidelining of women's contributions to the field. While there have been impressive women artist-directors like Shobhana Samarth during this time, the output and impact remain limited and difficult to source.[31] It felt important to us to locate contributions by women to visual culture in mainstream non-directorial roles, and hence emerged the third chapter on the actor Nutan and her crafting of visual and performative dynamism. The chapter starts with an early film in Nutan's career—Amiya Chakrabarty's *Seema* (Limit/Horizon, 1955) and traces Nutan's responsiveness to the cinematic frame to later, more complex articulations of her craft in the films *Sujata* (1959) and *Bandini* (1963). As Bimal Roy directed these latter films, our effort is to simultaneously examine his acute film-making sensibilities (defined by his training and experience as a film editor, including in *Mahal*) and to track what Nutan brings to Roy's *imaginaire* through her modulated performances.

The actor-director Guru Dutt was a starting point for this project and continues to inform the argumentative core of this book—even to his long-term associates and contemporaries, such as Abrar Alvi, Guru Dutt stood out for his implacable crafting of each separate image.[32] The angst-ridden artist who is more valuable dead than alive in *Pyaasa* (The Thirsty One, 1957) and the artist who is doomed to professional and personal failure in *Kaagaz ke Phool* (1959) were subject matters that made possible an incredible density of greys and the dramatic play of light, shadow and dimension. In many ways, several of the frames from these films, as lit and shot by cinematographer V.K. Murthy and as presented by the gravitas of Guru Dutt's acting and direction, have become emblematic of a stylised black and white aesthetics of Hindi cinema—this constitutes the fourth chapter of the book.

The discussion is continued in the fifth and final chapter with the elaborated cinematic layering of *Sahib Bibi aur Ghulam* (Master, Mistress and Servant, 1962), directed by Abrar Alvi and produced by Guru Dutt who also plays the protagonist. Several of the concerns that we have been tracking in the preceding chapters come together for us in this exquisitely constructed film—the architectural overtones of Kamal Amrohi, the inbuilt tautness of passion in Raj Kapoor's cinema, the precision of Nutan's performance under Bimal Roy's direction, and the gutted personal and social world of Guru Dutt. To this is added Abrar Alvi's panorama of tragedy encapsulated as pure lyric visuality. The Conclusion seeks to consolidate the insights of the book by surveying certain influential films and directors outside the purview of this book—their visual language no doubt contributed to the films discussed here.

In our readings of these films, we have chosen to work our way from within the film-text, looking at the construction of the visual aesthetics through the telling detail—the modes of structuring the plot, the dynamics of the *mise en scène,* the lighting of the frame. While we are cognizant of the historical contexts and thematic overtones, our methodology is more aligned to that of close reading. We have selected certain scenes that are sympathetic to our central insight(s) for each chapter, often moving from shot to shot and frame to frame, such that we are able to trace the film-maker or performer's line of thought and engagement. Through these 'micro-viewings', which at times might be the sequence or transitions of visuals or at other times a single piercing detail in a fleeting frame, we are underlining our conviction in the necessity to read film-text in an immersive mode, from inside-out and at the same time draw attention to the multi-branched ways in which affect is constructed as a whole. One has to negotiate the inevitable fact that a printed book like this necessarily reduces the aesthetic of movement (finely carved, phenomenological micro-aesthetics of shots and sequences) to stillness and sets of still photographs. Therefore, the inclusion of images in the book is not merely to illustrate our point but to invite readers into a direct engagement with the lexicon of the image and thus with black and white cinema on its own terms of stillness, vigour and movement.

As with any self-respecting mainstream film in India, we have felt reluctant to think of this work as belonging exclusively to any one genre, to be speaking only to one type of audience. Taking a cue from the oeuvre of film scholars-curators-practitioners, such as Annette Insdorf and Susan Sontag, we have attempted to write a book that will hopefully advance discussions in academic circles as well as invite the pleasure of a wider discerning audience. Perhaps some of these predilections come from the nature of aesthetics itself—its amenability to theorisation and abstraction but also its commitment to crafting the possibility of hedonist submergence. After all, this is the sort of collective sharing that can only happen in large dark halls, when the lights go out, the screen turns pale and the projector starts to run.

Overture: Kamal Amrohi's *Mahal* (1949)

There are few directorial debuts and opening sequences in Indian cinema to match the creative audacity of Kamal Amrohi's *Mahal* (Mansion, 1949). From the opening bar of music, the viewer sinks into a tapestry of seemingly incompatible elements—the materiality of wealth, the ethereal shadowiness of the supernatural, the quest to resist and detonate clock time, the endless reclaiming of a relationship that is destined to play out in that lost dimension of time. The only way this immersion is sustained, made credible and palatable to the audience is through a finely etched lyricism that has been shot and edited with an intuitiveness that deserves closer analytic attention than received so far.

Mahal was a commercial success that left a lasting imprint on popular culture, especially with Lata Mangeshkar's song *Aayega aanewala* (the one destined to come will come) which Majumdar marks as 'the transition from "ghost voices" [of barely known musicians] to the aural stardom of "playback singers" a transition forced by fans'.[1] Scholars have often read the film in the genre of the gothic[2] and there is enough to support that reading—from the architectural to the supernatural to the atmospheric. The film also pays tribute to the *noir* genre—the dark (trench) coats and hats, the evocative music, the watchful eyes, the defined shadows. If one looks at the features of melodrama offered by Ravi Vasudevan—the emphasis on loss, difficulties of achieving romantic fulfillment, high contrivance in narrative mechanism like coincidences—then *Mahal* would fit the bill.[3] However, the film defies a facile genre ascription, and is instead a composite of many forms, including thriller, horror and romance, as Rachel Dwyer points out.[4] Romance makes for a good inception point for our approach if we borrow from Barbara Fuchs's study of romance as both a genre and as a set of literary and textual strategies that can be adopted by different forms—'narratological elements and literary topoi, including idealization, the marvelous, narrative delay, wandering and obscured identity'.[5] In adapting many of these topoi to the Indian milieu, the film is a love story between two individuals thwarted repeatedly over lifetimes, and thus *Mahal* brings together romance and architecture on screen in a way that is distinctly its own. The dynamics between romance *and* space is also the romance *of* space, and the only way to bring it to any cinematic fruition would be to give that interplay of romance and space a unique visual syntax. This is what *Mahal* accomplishes with uncanny exactitude for the entire duration of the opening sequence.

As with any Overture, this section hopes to set both the mood and mode of close, shot-by-shot reading that will recur in this book. Equally, we are consciously working with a fragment of the filmic text, for often it is the telling fragment that can function as synecdoche. As influential film scholar Annette Insdorf writes in *Cinematic Overtures*,

> Gifted directors know how to layer the first shots in a way that prepares for their thematic and stylistic approach. Sometimes the opening sequence is intentionally misleading, inviting the viewer into active participation with the film, alert to the images and the sounds that will be developed through subsequent scenes.[6]

The effort is to interweave and establish a sympathetic common ground between the reading of the architecture of the cinematic/visual compositional style crafted by the film, with the architecture of space that is captured and projected on the screen.

From the credits, the idea and visualisation of architecture is given centre stage—the title of the film, *Mahal*, directly placed on top of the mansion it is referring to impresses upon the viewer an urgency and foreboding. The titles run on a painted backdrop that borrows directly from (and, in fact, replicates) the theatrical practice of the time. It evokes the grandeur of the historical or the epic. The screen is filled by three large buildings placed in a diagonal row; the distances of the grounds suggested in their diminishing size, and the tallest building at the left topped by a clock tower that will remain the dominant visual and affective trope for the rest of the film. The architecture signals various loaded semantics—Indo-Islamicate, Rajasthani and colonial. There are cenotaphs and pavilions, domes and commemorative spaces for the dead—this last is especially appropriate considering the centrality of the theme of death and rebirth. This theme of death operates at different levels. At first encounter, the plot of the film involves a romance with a seemingly other-worldly being. However, it may be said that that the storyline also signifies the deaths caused by the Partition of the subcontinent, as well as the death of a powerful South Asian Islamicate culture. M.K. Raghavendra writes of the cinema of the 1950s as specifically allegorising the nation as 'a palace or a residential building of prodigious proportions—and more enduring than its occupants—and that also becomes a site of intense conflict' and gives Amrohi's *Mahal* as an example.[7] Likewise, Dwyer has also written of the possible influences of *Rebecca* (1940), *Wuthering Heights* (1939) and *Citizen Kane* (1941) on the shooting of large, palatial houses with their decaying Gothic notes.[8] Perhaps as a testament to the conflicts of the past, the most visually arresting scenes are indeed those shot within the hauntings of the mansion.

But first, the transition from the outside to the inside needs to be negotiated. The film's titles fade out to a black frame and hand the affective baton to sound—a baritone male voiceover begins to narrate, 'Thirty years ago, on a stormy and rainy night…' At this, the viewer is returned to the same frame, the same perspective, as the title-sequence. However, the flattened backdrop has been replaced by a three-dimensional model of the same three buildings, now placed within an onslaught of wind, rain and lightning. The image dissolves into eye-level perspective, the camera directly behind a man in a trench coat pushing open the gates to the mansion (Fig. 1.1). The viewer is immediately invited into a tense and anticipative visual pacing vis-à-vis the immobile and daunting structure.

Fig. 1.1 Source NFAI

The cinematography and editing (by Josef Wirsching and Bimal Roy, respectively) animate the architecture, make it breathe, pause and then exhale. The film plays with light and form, the interior and exteriors of the house, the clock-towered mansion itself standing on a riverbank. A more ancient, 'feudal' and harsh order is evoked—not only are lovers unable to unite but that inability has much to do with opulent houses, the air of decay, haunted ghosts of frustrated love (Chapter 5 in this book—on *Sahib Bibi aur Ghulam*—again discusses such elaborate interior houses). Interiors are whole worlds. Hence, they are shot in a mode that is lyric, ornate and always crumbling—reincarnation seems natural here, in such a past-haunted world. The outdoor-garden is enclosed from public view and is thus more of an inner courtyard. On one side of the house is the river; the courtyard space contains large, erratically sprouting central fountains (as also in *Sahib Bibi aur Ghulam*) but keeping with the more Islamicate accent, in this film, there are also structures reminiscent of cupolas, octagonal/latticed columns, pillars with stone brackets and a freestanding multistoreyed pavilion frequented by the luring female protagonist who is implied to be a spectre from a past life. She is the one who sets the reincarnation plot in motion.

Mahal invokes the Taj Mahal, the world's most famous domed mausoleum. What precipitates the film is not so much an orienting shot but a stylised frame that gives the viewer a point of entry to the space through the silhouetted figure. The authorial voice that triggered the narrative by evoking a night of rain and storm continues to tell the story of this mansion—named *Sangam Bhawan* (a name that translates into 'house of union')—that has been desolate and abandoned for decades. It is important to note that after this initial orientation, the film will never return to this authorial voice. The establishing shot holds steady as the man in the coat, his back to the viewer, walks up the pathway from the spiked iron gates to the door of the mansion (Fig. 1.1). The setting is unpeopled but for the unhurried stranger. The sound of the wind carries a tension that is in conspiracy with the sonorous narrative, thus bringing forth an aliveness, an excitement. It is a low-lit atmosphere, attuned to the pacing of the protagonist's walk and with the narratorial voice explaining the mansion's desolation—the mansion is believed to be haunted by a boat that appears and drowns in front of it on rainy nights; this drowning is then followed by the sound of someone crying from within its walls.

At the end of this establishing shot that lasts for a dramatic minute and five seconds, a gardener appears from the background to light the protagonist's way and open the heavy, imposing, static door. The gardener takes over from the authorial voice and continues the strange story without missing a beat. In fact, as the authorial voice trails off with the line—'A very woeful love story took place here'—the gardener's voice responds—'Yes sir, in this mansion, a very woeful love story took place.' The triumph of this shot is as much in this seamless handing over of the storytelling baton, as in the shift of voice being in perfect empathy with the accompanying visual. The slow tracking shot moves through a doorway of the inner hall of the mansion, closer and closer to the gardener who is lighting the candle chandelier that has been pulled down to his level. The shot is in perfect opposition, and yet closely aligned, with the opening exterior shot. While initially the viewer was pinned to a wide establishing shot with the protagonist moving away, this is the moment of intimacy and mobility for the viewer who is suddenly on a fluid glide that takes them into the interior of this structure, closer to the storyteller and to the lighting taper that dips its flame into one of the glass casings of the chandelier (Fig. 1.2). Through this track, the viewer's vision dims in and out (the screen goes to black) to mimic the flickering of the candle.

Fig. 1.2 Source NFAI

The camera turns static for the next frame (Fig. 1.3). The lit chandelier is in the low foreground, the stranger-protagonist with his back to us takes off his coat and flings it. He pushes his hands in his pocket and starts to walk towards an arched doorway whose doors are swinging in the hinges to the sound of wind and the continued narration of the ghost story by the gardener. The gardener's voice picks up on the precise note of the words '*gumnaam shaks*' (nameless person) who built the mansion for a beautiful woman.

Fig. 1.3 *Source NFAI*

There is thus established in the film a folklore of death and grief, of ill-fate, of lost love—but instead of a rural setting with rural characters, the protagonist is in a trench coat, and this, in India at least, is of the world of the educated and urban elite (soon he will be introduced as a lawyer named Hari Shankar). While the protagonist is dressed in the manner reminiscent of a noir film, he is not in an urban crime scene but rather in a lonely, unpopulated house without clear reference to any city or village. It may be recalled that '[noir] is distorted angles, chiaroscuro lighting, and elongated shadows … urban realism, moral decay and sexual temptation'.[9] In some contrast, in this film, the hushed voice prioritises the folklore of the past—the house still seems a set piece of theatre with its large interiors and chandeliers. It will only fully come alive when the ghost appears. Something of that ghostliness is already present when Hari Shankar enters the house—with the slow track of the camera there is a new consciousness of space and movement. The darkness is played with—there is the storm outside and the lighting (lamp by lamp) of the chandelier within. The overall tension and energy picks up in the house. The self-referential camera marks two notions of architecture—one of the interior darkness of space and the other of the visual patterning of light (chandelier light as it appears and disappears off profiles, turbans and swinging doorways).

The still, anonymous protagonist who has taken off his coat is attentive (listening to the legend of the house at the same time as the viewer) to the unhurried rhythm of the story as it unfolds amid the sound of a storm and the light of the chandelier. His is an imposing, forbidding presence. The camera is much more sympathetic to the shapes of the mansion, such as the many fluted arches. Instead of revealing the protagonist's face, the chandeliers and mirrors obscure and defer the reveal, making him also seem as spectral as the tale, his anonymity now continuous with the story of the lovers.

The prominence of the reflective surfaces is crucial in the next shot (Fig. 1.4)—a wall-size mirror makes it possible to see the chandelier-lighting gardener from both front and back. As the listening protagonist moves closer, the camera does something uncharacteristic to the eye-level perspective maintained so far. It now sits below the chandelier, looks up at the gardener and his lighting taper, a tightly framed shot that allows for a sharp accent on the speaker's glance (Fig. 1.5). The face of the trench-coated protagonist has been kept tantalisingly inaccessible to the viewer, even as it has long been accessible to the gardener. The lighting taper in the gardener's hand moodily slides across the frame. This is even as the listening continues to bond the viewer to the protagonist.

Fig. 1.4 *Source NFAI*

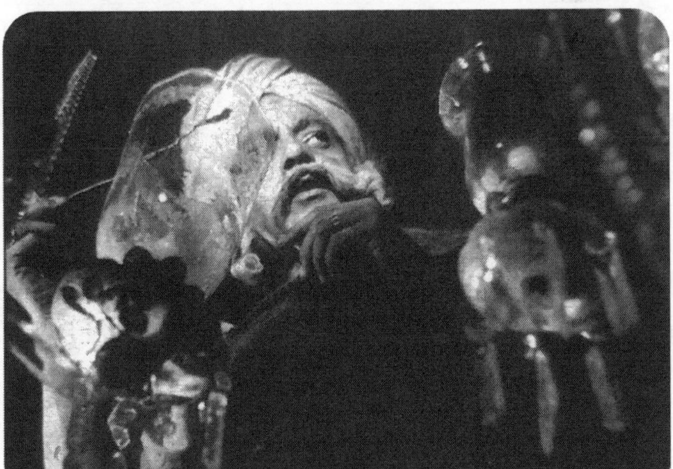

Fig. 1.5 *Source NFAI*

The resolution of this hide and seek of candles, shadows, silhouettes and mirrors is accomplished in one of the most evocatively choreographed visuals of the film—this is the next shot of the sequence. The viewer has been disoriented from the '180-degree axis rule' by (a) the round chandelier, (b) the moving storyteller (gardener) and (c) the giant mirror, and the shot places the viewer at an undefined spot in the room. Then the gardener blows up his taper and moves around to grab the chain that will lift the now fully-lit chandelier back to the ceiling (Fig. 2). The heaviness of the chandelier makes this a dramatic pulling that requires the man to bend his back and pull down the metal chain with all his strength. The pulley starts to work, the chandelier starts to rise, as the narrating gardener says, '…love has not failed and never will'. And just then, in perfect synchronisation to the affect and action, the camera starts to track in. The strength of the visual impact is heralded, on the one hand, by the tension of the rising chandelier slicing the vertical axis of the frame and, on the other hand, the tracking camera slicing the horizontal axis. At the centre of these two axes, the face of the protagonist is revealed for the first time. The camera continues to take us closer to him, with familiarity, curiosity and warmth. The full dramatic potential of the visual aesthetics of the film is concentrated in that moment.

Fig. 2 *Source NFAI*

Such stylised reveals and staging of the first glimpse of a star actor on the screen in every single film is a distinct characteristic of Indian mainstream cinema, something that the audience very much anticipates, looks forward to and often bursts into visceral celebrations in the cinema hall.[10] The star, in other words, debuts on the narrative canvas of the film as if it were their first career appearance but always with the confidence of being an established, celebrated artist. Here, the protagonist is played by Ashok Kumar, who was then already a successful star of Hindi cinema and also the producer of the film. *Mahal* is, therefore, participating in that tradition of celebrating the first reveal of the star in a film, but the gothic overtones are pushing it in another direction—into an obscuration between the corporeal and the shadowy, the living and the dead.

This particular shot that catches the pulse of the opening scene ends only when the storyline of the gardener concludes with the death of the woman in his love story, the protagonist now fully visible to us without the obstruction of the gardener or the chandelier. He is sitting in a classic portraiture pose, body slightly angled in a straight-back chair, an unlit pipe in one hand, a lit match in the other, frozen as in a painting. Both viewers and the protagonist are now in possession of the mysterious story. All that remains of that love story is the space and air of the mansion, its swinging doors and fluttering curtains—these keep the house alive, evoking desire and lost love.

The protagonist sends the gardener on an errand and starts to retire into one of the rooms—the lens wide enough to capture the breadth and height of the room—when a large painting drops from the wall. It narrowly misses the protagonist, who is startled and comes back to investigate. What follows is a slow process of shock and recognition: the film achieves this by first concentrating on the soundscape (the wind outside turning eerie) and a lengthy shot that is choreographed again to the affect of the reveal—a close reaction shot of his eyes opening wide and him moving back. The shot continues with a tilt down to his feet and then pans with the feet as they walk slowly to the left of frame, till the cinematic frame touches and overlaps the frame of the fallen painting. In the same shot the man's hands come down on the artwork—it is a portrait that looks exactly like the protagonist except for moustache and beard. The viewer is again encountering a mysterious piece of the story at the same time as the protagonist as they watch the portrait from over his shoulder. He bends down to the canvas, touches it with his left hand, the portrait now a faux looking glass. We dissolve to a similar frame, and the camera tracks back—the viewer's eye has been moved spatially without any time lapse (Fig. 3). The portrait is now propped against a wall, the man faces the painting just like the viewer and the camera tracks back to reveal a large old wooden, pulsing grandfather clock.

Fig. 3 *Source NFAI*

The presence and function of clocks in the film is one of its most prominent and sustained tropes—its ringing is often a punctuation of memory and desire. Certain times, such as 2 am, are shown to be more propitious for the otherworldly love story to unfold. Rachel Dwyer writes of the uncanny in *Mahal*, a fear of objects that becomes almost anthropomorphic and which she locates in the clock and the film's obsession with doubling, a common feature of the uncanny.

She reads the clock's striking of two as continuous with the many doubles in this story about reincarnation.[11] In the following frame, a taut triangle is formed of man-portrait-clock, and the clock strikes just as the protagonist asks the portrait—'Could it be that I am you, reborn?'. The triangular *mise en scène* (of the two selves and the clock) is 'interrupted' by a female singing voice that expertly picks up the cue of the beating clock. It is a haunting opening refrain of a song. This entire opening scene has now run for a little over ten minutes of screen time. The scene with its tightly conceived visual units and their modulated transitions has sustained a hypnotic line of narrative composition that is in conspiracy with the capaciousness of the house. This conspiracy can only be breached by a different cinematic element—here, it is finally and effectively breached by an amplified soundscape of clock and song. While the film began with a stylistic indebtedness to Hollywood noir, with the introduction of this sound, the visual treatment shifts to the more conventional idiom of romance.

As the phrases of music swell, the man turns and huge heads of shadows tremble outside the glassy door—the door opening is timed to shifts of music. Shadows of a large plant flit on his face, only the moving whites of his pupils unblemished by the shadowy light. He walks slowly; though the voice is spectral, nothing yet marks the moment as dream or memory-stalked or in any way otherworldly, except the gardener's story. Bimal Roy's clean, unhurried editing allows the slow unfolding and inhabitation of the space. The female singing voice has no clear location and he moves uncertainly, ascending staircases, looking up and down. There seems to be a silence in his movement that enfolds the music—it is silence that is the contribution of the black and white film and Roy's editing with those extra lingering seconds on many shots enhances that sense of ethereality. Equally, the camera treats the set as an older architectural grandeur, taking the spaces within as serious and delicate, giving importance to the verticality of the structures (stairways, fountains, arched pavilions, all often shot in reverential low-angle). The lip-synch tradition of the voice in Indian cinema allows it to float—a voice not clearly located in a figure or throat on the screen. The film plays with the spectrality of voice, and the success of the song has been attributed not only to its ethereality and mysteriousness but also because 'its purity and unearthliness was ideally suited to the haunting songs'.[12] The storm outside is temporarily hushed—the song makes what could simply be a large, inert house come alive. At one point (in the elevated yet still diegetic space of song), a large shadow moves past portrait and clock.

The female protagonist Kamini (played by Madhubala, then still in the early years of her career) first appears as this large shadow that skims over the ominous clock, continuing the theme of elusiveness. On her appearance, the glass chandelier with its many lit flames starts swinging wildly. The first frontal lit shot of Kamini—in an aureole of light from the candle she carries as she walks down the stairs in a dark sari (Fig. 4)—is in contrast to Ashok Kumar's first reveal that has been discussed. This time, the viewing is not shared with another character (such as the gardener) but is exclusively for the viewer. Kamini's potential paramour is still searching the house not knowing what she looks like. The viewer's active participation in the pact of the house and the ghostly romance is sealed.

Fig. 4 *Source NFAI*

There is sumptuousness in the slowness of the song that we hear (*Aayega aanewala*). The camera is sympathetic to Kamini's privacy and the moments of the discovery of her presence are through discreet glides and slow pans. The camera is also sympathetic to Hari Shankar's ghost-struck movement and his attempt to slowly unravel the mystery that he already suspects to be one of reincarnation. He is not horrified or terrified by this woman's spectral presence, but only searching for the truth—the discovery of the painting has made him determined to find the truth of his previous life. The camera is also searching and is interested in Hari Shankar's searching. The pace of searching precludes the genre of a thriller and is instead a supernatural, paranormal romance (the otherworld seen through delicately backlit *jaalis* or latticed windows). Kamini's beauty (*kamini* can be translated as 'the lover' or as 'beautiful woman') is not of the genre of horror either (the viewer does not get the sense that her real body is, say, Kali-like) but rather her beauty subtler, of a veiled luminous core. The lighting cannot be fully realist—it was supposedly night when the film began but now we are in an indeterminate lighting space and the sources of light on the screen cannot exactly capture the light values we see (for example, her face as she moved down the stair cannot actually only have been lit by one candle). The voice ends on a long shot of a silhouetted figure in a boat rowing down the river.

In defiance of spatial and temporal laws and to the consternation of both the protagonist and the viewers, Kamini reappears mysteriously in the house and the camera continues to play with this blocking and unblocking of Hari Shankar's vision (through arches, stone *jaalis*, pillars, garden plants). The storm is over, it is hushed, and there is a ghost in the house. The viewer sees for the first time Kamini's full gaze at Hari Shankar, again through the *jaali*—though even here the camera aligns less with their gazes and points of view and more with the structures and spaces of the house. Inverting the more classic 'male gaze' on the elusive woman, here the architecture of the house with its latticed windows not only enable her to meet his gaze but to return the look with frank unapologetic interest and desire—cinematically, he is left unaware of the assertive desire of her gaze.

The spell of the house and her hovering gaze can only be broken by the intrusion of an outsider—here it is Hari Shankar's sceptical friend—and by the possibility of violence. Hari Shankar pulls out his gun in fear and later his friend fires a bullet at the apparition, only to hit one of many mirrors. There is suddenly an indeterminacy of space, image and embodiment. This spell breaks due to two reasons: (a) when the friend tells Hari Shankar to leave the house and (b) when Hari Shankar speaks to Kamini. Thus, it is language and space that shatters the bewitchment. Following this, 'the ghost story' will exist in the rest of the film in a less striking manner and only as an explicit plot thematics of romance, instead of the lavish interplay of lighting, space and silence in these initial scenes.

There is, however, a memory of this first quarter of the film in a later song (*Mushkil hai badi mushkil*). Kamini is singing of *viraha* (the absence of the lover) and the wind is different from the first sequence—there is no roar, it is much quieter, the curtains flutter less. The house and air thus take on the shape of the camera's affect. Ghosts, in their longing, are very much rooted to local land and riverscapes—one desires not only the partner but also a native milieu. Ghosts always seem to inhabit only places of beauty—architectural and natural places that seem to have an apartness, a sense of ruin.

As Hari Shankar gets more and more mesmerised by the beautiful apparition, his friend badgers him into leaving the house for it is the house that is seen as '*manhoos*' (inauspicious), and whether they believe in the existence of the ghost or not, it is clear that the house is not separate from Hari Shankar's obsession with Kamini. It is only when Hari Shankar leaves the house for the station that we get our first visual of an urban public space—he is at the Allahabad railway station. Allahabad, celebrated for its confluence of rivers and known in Sanskrit as Prayaag, is a site that invites viewers into many layers of history, including rich Islamicate and colonial histories. As the landscape rushes past the train window, it includes the imposing outline of the mansion against the horizon. This view from the train is a vantage the viewer has not had thus far—we see a tall structure with three arches, an imposing clock tower, stacked windows and a pavilion overlooking the river. All the rooms of the house are mysteriously lit—the camera returns to Hari Shankar for a long reaction shot. One recalls the key reaction shots of three important first glimpses—of the painting, of Kamini and of the house. The mansion is now seen as a whole, having a meaning for him that it could not have had when he last saw it at the very beginning of the film as he walked up the pathway. The view of the clock tower triggers the sound of two gongs followed by the familiar song (regarding the promised return)—perhaps it plays only in Hari Shankar's head but it is objectively present to the listeners too. The use of the image and ticking of a clock make possible an intuitive transition from one space to another (all houses have clocks) and further, the stroke of a clock aurally mirrors a heartbeat. The melodic line of this song is never far from any event in the film—it can be picked up at any time. According to scholars, it was in the 1940s that the film song came to be separable as a sequence but Mahal harks back to the earlier age when songs always seemed woven into the plotline.[13] Hearing the song, Hari Shankar is inexorably pulled back. Unable to bear, after the haunting voice, the prosaicness of the sounds of the train (and the larger mundanity of his life), Hari Shankar returns to the house to encounter yet another vision of Kamini on the swing with the same song.

Though the second inning at the mansion is not as evocative as the opening thirty minutes of the film, a few further layers in the use of space and movement are revealed. Hari Shankar is silent as he approaches Kamini, his intense eyes are fixed on her, moving closer, as she swings gently, the camera cutting between his silence and her staccato speech—'You are back? I knew you would come back. Why do you look so surprised? I am not an illusion. I am not a dream. Look at me closely. Don't touch. Only look at me. Talk to me. Who are you?' There are no more visual tricks—both characters are illuminated and exposed to the viewer's curiosity and the repeated invitation to look (by Kamini) underlines the import of what the frame can offer and make concrete, especially when everything is at risk of being dismissed as illusion and dream (or poison, as the friend calls it). This moment is interrupted by the returning friend's voice—he had suspected that Hari Shankar would not be able to resist the lure of the house or the romance.

In the visual threads that follow this intrusion, Kamini seems to move in a truly spectral way through the inside and outside of the house, suddenly appearing in the domed pavilion by the river, in the doorway and mid-stair and threshold, as well as the upstairs and downstairs of the house. This is continuous with later treatments of their meetings—the house is revealed to be labyrinthine, full of secret interior tunnels and towers with winding stairways. The rest of the film sustains this treatment of space and longing. Only Kamini knows the way around the mansion, leading Hari Shankar through the many hidden rooms and stairs and it is as they walk thus that she narrates the story of their past life. Many of these stairs and cellars serve as both transitional and narrative spaces, and she is talking too of the transitional spaces between life and death, of deaths trapped within space and time (here, in cellars and attuned to the striking of the clock). Moving down the stair, Kamini is herself a wavy light (contoured by candle, face, fabric and jewellery) in a black frame. It would seem that ghosts can navigate such houses better than humans. The interiors of the mansion are not passive but serve as surfaces and obstacles for the otherworldly lighting. Kamini is elusive and seductive. She says she is leading him towards his death, and this journey to the underworld is spatialised as a dark descending and ascending of stairs, uterine, winding, with shadows that dwarf the humans who cast them. Hari Shankar is exhausted, anguished, sweating, bleeding (he falls and hurts himself while searching for her). Her voice directs him, telling tales of love and previous births—he is so hypnotised by her voice that he does not reach out to touch her even though she is close. Each frame with its dark outlines and slivers of light install the viewer deep in the space, an inhabitation that aligns us with the possibilities of this mortality-defying love story.

We are an hour into the film (the total duration is close to 150 minutes) when the solution to this haunting that plays out in the confines of the mansion is categorically disrupted. This can only come from the social and the filial—the intensely personal and erotic in opposition to the norms of the dutiful Indian family. Hari Shankar's father arrives at the mansion, takes his son away and persuades him to marry another woman. Through this 'crisis of his masculinity'[14], Hari Shankar attempts to move on with his life but the beating/striking of clocks, even in a distant land, puncture the consummation of his marriage, forcing his mind to transition back to the mansion and the older unconsummation. The *mahal* in this latter part of the film is only by suggestion or in a distant parallel world. However, the resolution of the narrative arc and its true anchoring can only happen in the mansion and so is plot-bound to return.

Hari Shankar is put on trial for complicity in his wife's death and the painful court proceedings become the space for unpacking the story from Kamini's point of view—she is now revealed to be the daughter of the mansion's gardener who used her familiarity with the mansion's spaces to concretise her belief that Hari Shankar was her lover from another lifetime. Kamini and Hari Shankar meet again in jail—he is behind bars. Aged by all the events, Hari Shankar wears a beard. In other words, he begins to look like the portrait of the opening sequence described earlier. It is only in this sequence—the latticed windows of the mansion replaced by the cold iron bars of jail (a different incarceration)—that the lovers are so close together in the frame that they can almost edge out the viewer's gaze.

Kamini has been revealed as human. Her love was not a lie, for indeed, how else could the domestic help have hoped to win the landlord's son? But even now their vision cannot fully find each other as the gaze is through prison bars. The prison cell is a frame within a frame, the gritty containment of the many deaths and rebirths that Hari Shankar whispers to her. We share his visual point of view of Kamini—the close-up is bordered by her dark shawl, her cheek balancing a single brimming tear.

Keeping with the melodramatic arc of the plot, Hari Shankar's execution is stayed by the state and he returns to the mansion, but he is too late to claim his love—at his insistence (during the jail meeting), Kamini has just married his friend. Hari Shankar accepts that this romantic deadlock is not meant to be resolved in this lifetime and dies in the chair placed strategically at the centre of the mansion's hall, similar to the shot that first revealed him to us. He looks ever more like the frozen, painted face of the portrait of the first scene. It is as if the portrait was not so much past life as a presentiment of the future. The promise of return is a circularity of time and image. The camera tilts up from the dead man to the silent tear-shedding Kamini now behind his chair (significantly, it is the first time their bodies touch), and then to the portrait high on the wall, all to the music of the song that had brought them together at the beginning of the film.

The last shot of the film is again another illustration of the sophisticated synchrony between visual, space and affect that was discussed in the opening sequence—the shot places the dead man in his chair in the centre of the mansion's hall and also in the centre of the camera's frame. The friend starts to walk towards the viewer and Kamini starts to walk in the opposite direction, her back to us, into the arched interiors with their evident depth of field. As the camera tracks back with the walking friend, it swings gently, as does the chandelier, the sensation of motion akin to the inside of a boat (the line of the song mimics this as it wonders when the boat of the heart will reach its shore—*na jane dil ki kashti kab tak lage kinare*). It is as if an eternal rhythm of time has taken over the mansion again, and their death is not so much tragedy as a romance that will consummate, albeit over a journey of several generations. As the friend exits the left of frame, the doors of the mansion slowly swing shut on the dead and the haunted living and the frame fades to black.

All the genre possibilities that have been associated with *Mahal*—thriller, gothic, horror, melodrama—melt down at this moment to the genre of romance. Fuchs' argument about the cluster of narrative strategies and recurrent traits that represent the genre-effects of romance are aplenty in this film—'delay and deferral, the pleasure of the reader, a fascination with female vulnerability, an emphasis on the marvelous over the quotidian, a focus on the travails of the individual, a nostalgia for other times and places'.[15] The mystique of architectural space and of (im)mortal love come together in a self-conscious exploratory style that aligns itself with romance—to this, one may add the specification of necrophilia, one further associated as much with half-lit face and voice, as with a haunted, immemorial house. *Mahal* embodies this definitive moment in Hindi cinema where there is an embracing of the romance of the visual—space is not just inert. Rather the medium of black and white helps emboss and literally immortalise loss and affect. The visual is able to carve a distinct romantic identity. This is not necessarily through themes or skillful plotting or brooding characters but by this aspiration of creating an entire, concrete visual sensibility that is a fulfillment of that romance, even as the plotline remains ostensibly 'tragic'.

At the end of this textual overture to the book, it is worth saying a little about the tradition of the overture in Hollywood cinema, as it travelled from the western classical music repertoire to the screen—essentially orchestral music played out against a black frame before the camera starts its work, a 'settling down' time for the audience as much as it was their 'mood setter'. The first 'talkie' *The Jazz Singer* (1927) featured an overture and the tradition continued sporadically for several decades. In *Gone with the Wind* (1939), the overture plays against a scenic still frame of the fictional plantation Tara (the film's investment, as indeed its female protagonist's, in the spatiality of large plantation houses is comparable with *Mahal*). In some ways, this narrative device before the start of the plot becomes the film's minus-zero time, a subterranean space that cannot quite be captured by the flash of credits that now open most films for us. Indeed, a year before *Mahal* was released, there was another debutant director whose film made astute use of this (pre-credits) space: he used it to foreground the trope of fire that is in the title, punning on fire as both traditional, appeasing Hindu sacrificial fire, but also, in the conflictual sense of the fire of creative and romantic passion. It is to Raj Kapoor's *Aag* that we now turn.

The Rebellious Image: Raj Kapoor's *Aag* (1948)

In 1947, as the country was grappling with the tumult of change and trauma, a young man in his early twenties was busy at work in the film studios—acting, directing and producing his first film. The film was released the following year and would mark the launch of a formidable career. Known for his convention-approved good looks (blue eyes, fair skin) and his performance-pedigree (his father was among the most reputed actors of the time), Raj Kapoor choreographed in his debut film *Aag* (Fire, 1948) the perfect act of rebellion, both in life and on screen. There are at least three concurrent rebellions to consider: (a) the character Kewal must rebel against a dominant father figure and against social expectations (a career on stage instead of in court as a lawyer), (b) the actor (Raj Kapoor) rebels by choosing to show his face on the screen for the first time not with an investment in the beauty of face and body but in the presentation of disfigurement—it is a burnt face lit up as grotesquerie—and (c) the director (Raj Kapoor) then matches grotesquerie to passion and performance to affect—again, not primarily through the storyline but through the insistent, reverberating trope of fire. This cinematic configuration of passion as a form of rebellion becomes embodied as visual and moral disfigurement through fire—fire is depicted as conflagration, destruction as well as sexual smolder. The protagonist's rebellion (his decision to be an actor against the wishes of his father) that plays out under stage lights and in the proscenium space becomes the vantage point from which this chapter proceeds.

More than any other figure represented in this book, Raj Kapoor has been acknowledged in the scholarship as not only a representative film-maker of the 1940s to the 1960s[1] but someone whose on-screen and offstage personae were symbiotic and continuous. Writing of Kapoor's relationship with the actress Nargis, Majumdar remarks that their 'on-screen identity functioned to overwrite, legitimize, and contain all extra-filmic information about them'.[2] Similarly, the off-screen details about Raj Kapoor—such as the well-known quarrels with his actor-father Prithviraj Kapoor, his refusal to study law and his choosing cinema[3]—are in line with the intergenerational father-son masculinist narratives that play out on the screen, not just in *Aag* in 1948 but it remains a dominant feature of Kapoor's oeuvre all the way to *Bobby* in 1973. *Aag* is about the struggle of the protagonist Kewal to be a theatre director; for this, he has to defy his family and undertake an arduous personal journey. The love for theatre is a long-standing friction from childhood onward, peppered with a corresponding romance for each stage (youth, college, professional) of his life. Kewal decides to find his way out of the family fold and after much hunger and despair, eventually finds patronage. When he has finally established himself as a director, even his conciliatory parents appear at the premiere. But in that premiere, Kewal and his theatre are engulfed in fire and he suffers burns on one side of his body and face. In despair over such a catastrophe, he agrees to an arranged marriage, only to find out that, fortuitously, the bride is his childhood sweetheart and fellow theatre-lover. Thus, a dream for theatre stirs again in both of them. The Oedipal tussle in *Aag* between father and son is also the battle between theatre and cinema. But there are no simple linearities or overturnings. *Aag* is cinema that valorises theatre, even as theatre itself as an independent aesthetic form seems to be dying—the theatre, after all, burns to the ground at the end of the film. The vanity and rebellion of the son also seem to be penalised by the burning of the face—'to blacken one's face' is a common Indian phrase to indicate shame and punishment. The film is a dark imagination of creativity and rebellion.

Raj Kapoor produced *Aag* (with V.N. Reddy as cinematographer) before he became a star and before he had any assurance of that stardom. The quest for success is represented in the plot of the film.

This chapter will also focus not so much on this explicit plotline but in the aspiration of the camera to shoot 'stardom'. In other words, the camera has to highlight the male actor not just as one element in a *mise en scène* but as the vortex around which the other cinematic elements have to be adjusted. This centrality of the hero, the heroic and the passion that comprises the substance of this heroism is distinct to Raj Kapoor. One says this because the heroism discussed in other chapters of the book (of Guru Dutt or Ashok Kumar) is more narrative or circumstance driven. In contrast, Raj Kapoor's heroism is driven by a more celebratory male embrace of screen visuality. The creation of a star-persona on screen necessitates a distinct stylistic idiom: There has to be a way to communicate the camera's rapture with the star. All props, spaces and actors on the frame must refer to him, even if he is not overtly in the centre of the frame. Conventionally, angles are picked that highlight the star's necessary beauty (the male jaw is strengthened or the female jaw is softened); lighting and posture must combine to flatter, the hair-lock must be trimmed and angled just so on the forehead. The camera is synchronised with the musical line that is in tune with the gait and voice of the star. Whatever the narrative exegesis (sorrow or joy, poverty or wealth), the icon of the star must be resplendent—sorrow or poverty adds to that resplendence as naturally as joy or wealth or romantic success. The 'humanisation' is for everyone else—for the star, the camera is never disjunct and the stitches and synchrony (music, image, narrative, the meaningful silence or pause) must be seamless.

And yet, for Raj Kapoor, this normative shooting of the star is one that must also be punctured before being redeemed. The rebellion is this moment of puncture—for example, as seen in the opening sequence, one that is self-consciously experimental. Instead of the reveal of the face of the star, we have a long sequence of walking feet—these feet guide our eyes up the stairway and towards the traditional posture of the waiting and expectant bride. What is revealed to us (and the bride) simultaneously is the tragedy of that very face—where there should have been beauty (and where there had indeed once been beauty), there are now only unbearable scars. This moment of the camera invading the privacy of the face (to reveal not expected beauty but repulsion) is the rebellion of the image, of the eye fighting itself.

The rebelliousness of the image takes different forms in Kapoor's work—it cannot be a coincidence that his first two films (*Aag* and *Barsaat*) are released within a year of each other and are named after fire and rain. The conflicts of identity, creativity and sexuality of the protagonists in both the films are displaced onto the pervasive symbolism of the elements. In some ways, doing this makes it possible for the director to escape the definition of individual passion entirely within a social paradigm and instead to stand for itself alone. The filial or social world, as significant as they might be in moulding the protagonist, is unable to contain the passion of these early films, a passion that overflows into more primordial realms. Invariably then passion has to recognise itself in an image—whether it is the tongue of fire or the torrent of water. The image has to burn through or submerge the frames of a conventional seeing.

The tempo for such an approach is necessarily high pitched and the first minute of Kapoor's first film is already an inferno—a climatic high note. The opening visual of the film's credits could very well have been its end credits—such is its spoiler-laden circularity. A still frame of the curtained stage of an impeccable proscenium theatre is visible to us for fleeting seconds before it is engulfed in smoke and flames—all to the music of frenzied strings and percussion in an orchestral arrangement that evokes the affect of drama and distress. The three alphabets that make the title of the film in English are also aflame—the dissolve retains the name of the main actors, whose names are now on fire. As we will discuss in this chapter, the only means to counter the restless billowing energy of fire in the film is the stately solidity of the theatre stage which forms the constant dark background of the credit sequence.

The credits (white script in Roman on a black background) are licked by flames and there is a flare of fire between subsequent frames of names. The music wavers, shifts to the tabla and shehnai (wind instrument associated with weddings) and the shots of the fire now evoke a wedding fire (even if at this point it would seem that the trope of the fire is too great to be contained in the highly codified social-ritual-legal wedding altar). There is the tension between the domesticated fire of ritual and the inferno engulfing the screen. The credits end with the music turning ominous, wild, jarring, unrestrained (that is reflective of the large-scale fire rather than the contained one). The stage is set for the screen debut of the director-actor Raj Kapoor.

The First (Un)Veiling

The first scene of *Aag* is unique for the care it takes in its simultaneous exploration of the many possibilities of veiling and unveiling (both literal as well as symbolic)—a bride will go through the traditional emergence from her bridal veil (to be gazed at by her new husband) and the husband carries his own veil of secrets (a disfigured face that his bride has not yet seen). The scene begins with a man's legs and feet—he is wearing a white, formal *churidar* (tight-fitting trouser). The camera pans and tilts with the torso-less body as it walks across the frame and up a flight of dark stairs, the meagre light reflected in the shiny surface of his *kurta* (loose collarless shirt), again signifying the ceremonial. The music drops to a somber staccato beat that synchronises with his moving feet. The second shot is of a dimly lit and shuttered wooden door—the viewer has reached it a second or so before the protagonist walks into the frame, back to the camera and slowly pushes the door open to the light of gossamer veils with the low lamps of a bridal chamber, the veiled bride is visible in the distance, framed through the protagonist's outstretched hand on the door (Fig. 1). He takes a couple of steps forward and the camera not only tracks with him but audaciously pushes through the gap of his hand, giving us a glimpse of the bride—the camera that moves past his hand thus reaches for an autonomy beyond his gaze and anticipation. This moving-past becomes a logical invitation to a mid-shot that looks directly at her in profile and the camera determinedly tracks ahead to a closer frame. The profile is of significance in this sequence because of the hide-and-seek affect it wishes to sustain, the split in the protagonist between unburnt and burnt, between past and present, between vanity and trauma, between despair and desire. The viewer's gaze cuts from the waiting bride's pristine profile to a mid-shot of the groom who has closed the door behind him (Fig. 2). His fine-featured profile is gently lit, though darkness continues to drape his shoulders and large shadows hover around him and the shuttered door. He breathes deeply against the door and the close-up of the bride that follows is now purely his point of view—we have turned into invisible voyeurs in the nuptial chamber.

Fig. 1 *Source NFAI*

Fig. 2 *Source NFAI*

When the viewer returns to the previous frame of the nervous bridegroom against the door, it is to witness deep stirrings of desire mingled with fear—he crushes a shawl against his chest, drops it and then the hand goes back to his collar, tugs at his own clothes. He gathers courage, begins to speak—the tone is of banter, of talking to oneself but it is also a lighthearted overture to his new wife. He complains about Kanhaiya (presumably the domestic help) who has put a pile of clothes and jewellery on his bed as if there were no other place—the bride reacts in shyness and moves slightly, as does a slightly wobbly camera, to which the new husband feigns surprise—'*Arrey*, this bundle has started moving!'—in a frame that is compacted to flatter his aquiline profile. The bride smiles bashfully under her veil as the protagonist's voice continues off-screen to say—'So there you are—Sudha … what a lovely name' (*sudha* means nectar, that which in Hindu mythology revives the dead and rehabilitates the demonic). It is a familiar moment—he on the threshold, attempting a nervous joke, she a bride in finery with her head bent, in an environment of netting, curtains, lamps and potted plants. It is a scene of the 'first night', common in Indian cinematic imagination, though here, there is maybe more tenderness and humour than might be expected. One may recall that in Indian mainstream cinema, the first night is particularly erotically charged—and this charge is rarely if ever, revisited. It carries an assumption of a summit and consummation of sex—there is no such assumed eroticism in even the second night of marriage! *Aag*, in choosing this first night narrative to disturb the conjugal, thus strongly subverts tradition—the erotic capital is easily fungible to disgust.

The protagonist continues to speak and explain what the word *sudha* means, slowly moving towards her, his silhouetted body occupying the left of the frame, the camera closely shadowing his walk, as his hands reach over to lift her veil. The hand that lifts the veil and faces the camera has a large scar but the moment is not long enough to register. The veil is rising, the eye of the camera stays on the silent bride, tracking around to give us a full glimpse of her nude face. She lifts her face but only for a split second before her palms rush to cover it. All this is still perfectly familiar, except that the audience has been given an opportunity to be cued by the burnt hand, to see something the bride does not see. Her palms are still covering her face, her fingers taper beautifully, her hands perfectly lit. She is a beautiful bride with unblemished skin, bashful posture, the flowers of her hair and wrist weaving a perfect garland.

The man banters that she is perhaps not comfortable with the electric lighting and so he turns, walks back to switch off the light—and there is a moment of near-complete darkness in the frame but the camera eye lovingly catches an attractively deep silhouette of him in a tapestry of shadow—the perfect stillness of blissful ignorance before the storm of knowledge the bride must face. Two quick intercutting shots follow as he speaks and moves to her. The camera is poised for the reveal as it looks down at the bride from over the groom's shoulder—he unveils her (again) and lifts her chin gently towards himself. This has been an extended action—veiling and unveiling and the bride (beyond demureness and smiling and though centrally placed in the room and on the bed) has not yet 'acted'—not just in terms of speech but even in terms of expressing desire beyond a sense of diffident complicity in his banter. Now, with his palms insistent on her chin, she is forced to look up and affirm acceptance and even desire—she has to finally *see*. She continues to delay, her face rising, but not her gaze which is still cast down. All these images are 'full-bodied compositions'—the frame accommodates several carefully placed non-human textures and shapes (bed, curtains, door, flowers and a lamp), even as it gives primacy to the substantiality of (youthful) human figures.

It is clear to the viewer by now that the suspense of the entire opening sequence rests on the averted (delayed) gaze of the bride. Her face fills up the screen. She raises her gaze as if she has no option left. The moment is slow and laboured—perhaps accentuated by a cut that does not match action or perspective but 'goes back' in time to repeat (and thus prolong and heighten) the gesture of looking up. The viewer continues to look at the bride from the position of the groom, the man's right (burnt) hand in the foreground. Even the viewer who had missed the burnt hand before now realises that something is very wrong and that the wedding night is finally being violently ruptured. Traditionally, this may well have been the first time the couple would have ever seen each other's faces—in the marriage ritual itself, the glance would have been hurried, distracted and without privacy. The moment of egalitarian partnership—partners gazing longingly into each other's eyes—is too bold within this inegalitarian context, where the man must hunt with his gaze and the woman must defer her's for as long as possible. Indeed the typical gesture would be the standing man finally prying open her fingers to see her face and she thus sees only because he wants to see—for her to have curiosity (even to her husband) and act on it would be too bold. She has to wait for him to insist on the mutual gaze. This convention is inventively used in this context of delayed seeing.

In the same close shot that started full of untapped teasing desires, the moving gaze is going to shift to an affect of horror and repulsion. As the bride finally catches a glimpse of her husband—not yet accessible to the viewer—there is a sudden unexpected widening of that eye and then an open-mouthed scream, her fingers leaping to cover her mouth. The scream is the climax of the scene, the pivot and reveal over which everything turns, thus transforming the expectation of the traditional wedding night scene. The next close-up is the one that the entire opening sequence has been anticipating—the hidden profile of the protagonist, the reason he prefers the dark, is now lit entirely from a low lamp beside the bed. The side of the face that the bride and viewer now see—the camera having jumped the 180-degree axis—is charred, his eyes wide open, his teeth barred like a cornered animal. At the sound of her scream, his hand angrily shoots up, creating a diagonal slash in the frame (Fig. 3). It is a moment of contrasts accentuated by the lighting: the fire that sanctifies marriage is also the fire that irredeemably singes. Kewal's beauty is rendered fragile, finite, foredoomed.

Fig. 3 *Source NFAI*

In that affecting cinematic moment, however, all that the protagonist deeply feared has happened and he says so, filled with shame, sorrow and regret. The music changes from the distorted, raucous orchestral outburst to the melancholic strains of a Rudra veena and the moment of violence has transformed into a visual plea for pity as the camera allows him speech—he says that what he had feared the most had happened. He turns away from his bride to the window and his words now correlate to the offering (in turns) of the unburnt and burnt profile to the camera. Much of the opening scene has been this play of light and skin. Kewal twists and turns, as if the agony of the situation is imprisoning: there is the straitjacket of the wedding night scene and the actor has to free himself of it. This twisting and turning—the first cinematic presence of Raj Kapoor as actor/director/producer—was to contribute something to Kapoor's signature performative style over the decades. More than any of his contemporaries, he was always leaning, almost leaping and writhing into the camera as in this early scene from *Aag*. Later sections of the book will discuss ideas of acting from the 1940s onward—but one can already see a certain hyperbolic style compared to the more dominant norm of the restrained actor (such as his peers Nutan, Dilip Kumar, Ashok Kumar, Guru Dutt and Balraj Sahni). Kapoor's performance of Kewal's vulnerability is also characteristic: There is such an immediacy of affect that the image overshoots the frame as if there is almost no reaction time. The relay of facial expressivity is seamless—his acting is an immediacy of face, lips, eyes, voice, cheekbone and brow.

The name Kewal represents the solitariness of the artist and creator. The solitariness is also a kind of inwardness. In *Aag*, they reflect the content of the dialogue/script—there is the happy fantasy of husbandhood and love contrasted with the impugnable destitution of his present state. If Kewal were not scarred, his joy on this wedding night with a beautiful wife would be faultless and their marriage night would only add to the cinematic tradition. Joy and beauty seem so near but he cannot touch it. He remarks on the difference between *surat* (the face as outer nature) and *seerat* (behaviour as inner nature). This contrast of the inner and the outer is a key organising trope of the film. With both eye and hand burnt, there is the dual sorrowful scepticism towards the possibility of livelihood, as well as the impossibility of making that joy happen as a work of the human hand (and in the theatre, the beauty of the face is as vital as the muscle of the hand). When the 'bad' side is lit, there are strong shadows indicating a depth of despair, a desire to hide and to annihilate oneself. The images play with the traditional binaries of good and bad, hope and despair, inner nature and outer experience, the heart's desire and the social ideal.

Raj Kapoor relentlessly mines the pathos of this wedding night through this shaming reveal of the male face. He weeps (the burnt face now in full steady view of viewer and bride) and tells his wife that he was not always disfigured. Even though the hero is shedding tears and the romance of the moment is shattered, the affect cannot (and does not) collapse into tragedy—this is neither the hero nor the anti-hero but rather evocative of a 'pre-hero', one who has to labour against the conventional (and now defeated) expectation of the audience. He has to earn his new heroism through analepsis or flashback—this is to be the unfolding of the film over the next two hours. As Kewal becomes the narrative voice of the film's story, the camera seizes its first escape from the claustrophobia of the nuptial chamber that has been stripped of any possibility of consummation. We see the protagonist from outside that space, through the frame of a window he opens, the camera sympathetically swinging back to him. He begins to itemise his regrets—if only he were not attractive, if only he were not attracted to beautiful women and (third and most importantly for the plot) if only he were not besotted by theatre.

Kewal's verbal invocation of the past dissolves into the images of the past and his voice helps the visual transition—to a ten-year-old, with his mother putting a mark on his face so that the evil eye would not befall him. There is the shared vanity of mother and son in beauty (along with the fear that that beauty may have an evil eye cast on it)—as the viewer knows has indeed happened. This mother-son pact is broken by the father's entry and the father's irritation about his tie not being ironed (she had neglected her wifely duties in favour of being the adoring mother). The son looks warily at the father who does not look at him but only at his wife. The ache for approval is what will shape his adult professional life—the counterpoint to adoration and beauty in Kewal's life is ambition and drive, to be validated by public acclaim. This is fated to play out through resistance to the patriarch and as/on a grand theatre—in full view of the world.

Flirtation of the Proscenium Arch

Aag is a persistent meditation on theatre—the proscenium, the stage, the lights, the curtains—as opposed to the interior, the 'going-behind' (this is because the traditional spatial metaphor of 'going within' is less intelligible in the explicitly visual idiom of film). It incites the film to travel to a plane behind rather than within, as we shall see in the constant invocation of frontality and the three-dimensional behind-ness in several of the scenes. The proscenium has been considered the closest that the theatre-stage comes to the film screen, since 'the upper and lower lines of the frame—the optic lines that constitute the stage—are raised to create a frame at eye level, much like the cinema frame'.[4] The emphatic curve of the proscenium arch, by virtue of its location between the spatial/performative depth of the stage and the anticipation/expanse of the audience, becomes a crucial visual cue to read *Aag*. It is equally a powerful metaphor within the film, a conscious mode of framing the dramatic moment to suggest both explicit theatricality (since the protagonist is obsessed with theatre), as well as cinematic inscape (for this theatre is now captured within the frame of cinema).

Jane Feuer in her study of Hollywood musicals explores how proscenium arches occupy an ambiguous position, especially in 'backstage musicals' (where the plot is about staging a production as is the case in *Aag*). The proscenium is perceived as a barrier to direct communication. Thus, many attempts are made to dispense with the stage altogether and thus *create* prosceniums or stage-like arenas in other non-theatre spaces.[5] For instance, the play in *Aag* is everywhere but in the play-to-be-staged. Much of the film is about the numerous attempts to make plays, the failures of those plays, and then the drama outside the theatre of the final fire that ruins the play when it is eventually staged. True action is elsewhere—has always been elsewhere; the theatre has missed the ebb of history—it is no longer the centre but a theme for the new medium of cinema, which is only embedded in other mediums. The play Kewal is obsessed with is not really the production at hand (it is too frontal, too surficial) but is rather the attempt to stage the play—this is the real play for the viewer. The true drama lies in the play behind the play—the scenes, for example, of exalted parting that will be described later in this chapter. The only way this conceit will sustain is if the proscenium arch is constructed elsewhere, in an unexpected space—for instance, lovers will meet under the (proscenium-like) arches of a college housed in a colonial building. This sequence of overlaps of stage and image will be unpacked further.

The context here is that Kewal, who is in college, has failed in the examinations. While other students are jostling to see their marks (this was to be a familiar sight in Indian colleges for several decades and whole futures hung on such pieces of paper), Kewal is nonchalantly standing apart, looking at the poster of an inter-collegiate dramatic competition. The play to be performed is *Shakuntala* written by Sanskrit playwright Kalidasa in the fourth century of the Common Era. It is perhaps India's most reputed and performed classical play—its plotline too consists of parted lovers and thwarted recognition. The poster of the play has only two names on the billing—Kewal and Nirmala. Nirmala is the college classmate who shares his love for theatre and is attracted to him. It is clear that while Kewal's back is to academics/examinations, his face is turned hopefully to the prospect of a theatrical career, one that he will share with the woman he loves. The next shot has him rushing down the stairs to his house, excitedly telling his sceptical father about the play

(*Shakuntala*) he will be staging that night. The stern image of the father slowly dissolves into a dark frame with strong highlights, an establishing long shot of a lover waiting at a deserted college (Fig. 4.1). Of course, it is almost impossible that a young couple in the 1940s would have a whole empty college to themselves—this would be a fantasy even today. One soon realises the visual appeal of colonial college architecture with its arches and pillars in the late evening light. Nirmala is darkly silhouetted in the building, its arches radiating light from within. There is the strong darkness of the pillars and the gathering night outside. Here we have a suggestion and re-creation of the proscenium arch—the viewer is reminded that the couple is supposed to be performing a play that night but no staging can match the dramatic weight of this meeting of lovers. This is impressed upon the viewer by the tone of the music and the visual presentation of the scene. But the 'barrier' of the proscenium when recreated elsewhere is particularly amenable (and set up) to be deconstructed, as we see in the next frame when the camera crosses over into the 'stage space'—Nirmala first has her back to us and then turns around to hide behind a pillar (Fig. 4.2). In breaking that arch, we are complicit in the mysteries and sorrows of the meeting.

Fig. 4.1 *Source NFAI*

Fig. 4.2 *Source NFAI*

The entry of the hero to the space of the meeting is a visual duplication of the frame where we glimpsed his waiting lover. As the sequence unfurls, this image becomes an anchoring and orientation as we return to it several times: for instance, when he runs up the flight of stairs looking for Nirmala. Although we know Nirmala has arrived before him, Kewal is uncertain and runs through this 'stage space' while she is still hidden behind a pillar. One hears jagged, grandiose music, a sense that something is wrong as Kewal keeps calling out her name, searching up and down the stairs. There are depths to be penetrated in the college as well as horizontalities to be traversed as he moves, anguished, from left to right of frame, a tiny lit figure, moving in the darkness of the space, a voice calling out a name. The framing of this corridor is still in the mode of the proscenium entrance—the camera tracks with Kewal's anxious feet, and then with his hurrying torso.

As it turns out, Nirmala is betrothed to someone else and has come to tell Kewal that she would be unable to act that evening or indeed ever after. While he is talking of the delay in the current play, the viewer slowly realises that this is both Kewal's and the viewer's parting from Nirmala. The college has become a charged theatrical space, a theatre outside the theatre, a proscenium where fates are sealed. She is more resigned and it is Kewal whose body and voice now represent that bursting of emotion—one sees Kapoor's acting at its most emblematic for this is the type of performance he thrives on. A thin, nervous body rushing through space, calling her name, a youthful, absorbed lover (this is in spite of there being no stated, admitted love between them, only togetherness as fellow theatre connoisseurs). There are continual movements from shadow to spotlight, with strips of light in the college as it stands, night-lit. Her face is always just these slivers of light as if an interior is being shielded from having to reveal pain. Half-faces framed by arches—she carries secrets and depths (of sorrow, of the helplessness of a woman forcibly betrothed) that he can only dimly comprehend. She is absorbing the fullness of this moment, a conflict between the mind and its registration on her body. She has been depicted as helpless: stepping into the light with bent head, not initially responding to his call and then stepping back in fright into the darkness, her face covered, defeated. She is retiring, in contrast to his faster movement and frenetic domination of space.

The camera follows Kewal in a long shot as he walks the length of the screen. In contrast, she advances gingerly towards the camera, a shot that highlights the elongated foreground of the college floor. Her utterance of his name is full of weighted anguish. He is caught off guard, turns to see her, one side of his face fully lit and a closer shot that follows a little later reminds us that the lit side is the one that had been presented to us as singed in the opening sequence. The sight of her standing in the dimly lit corridors is now his point of view as he runs to her. But she is still, the weight of darkness heavy at her feet. The ill-fated couple separated by geometric patterns of shadow that cut into the night and the architecture of the college corridors now meet in a long shot, facing each other—the viewer sees them in profile (Fig. 5). They are centred in the frame and in the foreground is that self-same arch, now visually unifying a couple who will soon part and also doubling up as the proscenium for this staged dramatic moment.

Fig. 5 *Source NFAI*

The over-the-shoulder shots that capture the conversation between lovers can now settle into a more conventional cinematic mode. As opposed to the initial frontality—the proscenium effect, their silhouettes against the bust of the college patron—the camera in the latter half of the scene is on the other side of the line of vision. We are not watching them in one-dimensionality as in a play but we also inhabit the space around them, listening intimately rather than distantly watching. The viewer shares the tension and the obscurity of the scene and their emotions—the silence, the cry of footsteps, the voice in shadow through muffled tears. The close-ups of her face (and her backlit hair) now catch her swinging in and out of the light, as well as catching her tracery of tears. Her parents had taken decisions about her marriage without her knowledge. The camera starts pulling back from them, as they both register disgust at her betrothed and his plans to take her away.

In this part of the scene, Nirmala is captured more arrestingly than Kewal. Her eyes are covered in darkness and only parts of her—the moving, uttering mouth and the mehndi-covered palms—are revealed. This is when she conveys the key news: that she is to be married. The mehndi palms evoke the first scene where Kewal's bride had covered her face. Here, Kewal is shot frontally, fully lit, in mid or close shot, to allow his heightened acting to unfold. The focus of the visual is here clearly on the male star. This is in contrast to the more subtle depiction of Nirmala's face, where the lighting and moving facial expression or turns of the neck, choked voice and hand gestures catch the play of shadow and light more ambiguously. Just like the classical play *Shakuntala,* they were supposed to be acting in at that moment—which too was about romance and misrecognition—but Kewal seems to misrecognise Nirmala as his Shakuntala. The rest of the film is the search for the original woman-figure of his childhood (childhood love is the only true adult consummation) but here the entire figure of Nirmala (as well as Kewal's later love played by Nargis) is understood only as a digression from that original quest for recognition of the old, first, true love. He will find her only at the end of the film (in terms of the benign telos of the film, this is already located in the first scene of the film—his bride turns out to be that childhood sweetheart). The circle is complete.

To return to the college scene: Nirmala comes to sit beside him asking that she be called Nimmi (again, the theme of recognition, of wearing the guises of selves and names, if only in deception and fugitively). He calls her Nimmi and recites the chant that he has offered every woman in his life—he wishes them prosperity and a joyous, untainted life.

The lingering shot awaits the completion of the utterance as she rises and moves away, a block of receding shadow as the camera moves ever closer to him till his face takes over the space of the frame. The last sentences are intercut between his face, her walking backward and then running—this is to the sound of plucked strings. The irony is that though he has just lost an actor for a college play and she has pledged herself to a husband, yet it is she who has to console him and plead with him to not be angry. He grandly wishes her well, saying that this is not so much her fate, as his ill luck. Both speak slowly and there is a sense of ineluctability, yet for the male artist, art is extended boyhood—the woman actor's fate is more an annihilation, an excision from the film itself. As Kewal utters her name for the third time, the frame dissolves from his face to an image of wedding musicians and festivities, celebratory crowds and of course more fireworks—fire (the *aag* of the title) as the celebration and solemnisation of marriage, as evoked in the opening scene. But this time it is Nirmala who will be scarred by the wedding fire.

Answering the Curtain Call

The genesis of passion for theatre, as with most *kunstleromans*, is located in the protagonist's childhood when ten-year-old Kewal would sneak out of his house to attend theatre performances (these are shown to be traditional mythological plays with painted backdrops). This is to be contrasted later with the more contemporary plays that Kewal will direct. He is accompanied by his childhood sweetheart who makes a pact to always act with him as they embark together on their artistic careers. This leads to the first production of the Kewal Theatrical Company (as reads the hand-painted banner over a makeshift auditorium in a cowshed-like space). While the children gather to watch the show, the young artist's efforts to maintain the proscenium structure is obvious—the shed is divided into three areas—with the young children sitting on crates, three bedsheets hung to create curtains and the performance space and then the makeup space behind the curtain. From the importance given by the children to the curtains—their sombre drawing and closing—it is clear that this space and act of negotiating curtains is what signifies theatre to the young audience and actors. Kewal's debut play is never staged, for his sweetheart, the lead actress, mysteriously leaves town. This story is the bedrock of the plot of the film and also Kewal's self-narrative of his artistic trajectory with its constant heartbreaks and obstacles. It perhaps is a factor in his decision to finally leave his parents and live on the streets, to struggle and pursue his art rather than to succumb to filial duty.

The next and most significant negotiation of curtain and proscenium is the story of Kewal finding a home in theatre. The sequence starts with a shot of the pavement and then Kewal's feet in worn-out sandals—shots of road and feet were to be made famous in later Raj Kapoor films such as *Awaara* (The Vagabond, 1951) and *Shree 420* (The Gentleman Cheat, 1955). Prefiguring these films is the consciousness already present in *Aag* of the outside (street) as a space distinct from and discontinuous with the home, theatre, college and even the wedding halls/temples. The outside (the street) is its own world—in *Aag*, the street is still seeking autonomy, is the space for dislocation but the home is not yet the street (as it is in *Awaara*). The home is still an interior, specifically the still fantasised and loved interiors (stage, green rooms) of theatre that the interiors of the house or the college do not provide. The shots of the road dissolve to the words that Kewal had told his father—'I want to search my own way'. Walking thus in the unprotected street, with these rebellious words ringing in his mind, Kewal's body enacts a jagged, defiant physicality despite or because of his hunger, homelessness and anguish. Sometimes it seems that it is a voice repeating what he had told his father (and perhaps himself numerous times) but sometimes it is also a voice that seems to be speaking from the far future, a voice meant to reassure him of the correctness of his decision to rebel. The wandering dissolves to a low angle of a church, the camera moving down from its summit and then sideways to him sitting unshaven under a tree. The voice has not stopped speaking, despite clear signs of Kewal's increasing exhaustion. The camera-gaze glides down a tall building that also looks similar to the church—there are panels of classical Greek sculptures and the building is of great height. The building is not a church but something equally imposing—a celebrated landmark of Bombay's history—the Royal Opera House. The visual rhyming with the church elevates the opera house to a similar calling and power. Kewal walks into the building, his back to us, in the slower gait of a tired man—he is greatly diminished both by the size of the opera house and the large, plying double-decker buses. City, livelihood and art all conspire to confirm his smallness in the scheme of things, his vulnerability to fate.

A closer look at the images in this sequence gives us a sense of how the rebellion of theatre in the plot is, in fact, a rebellion of cinema in the amplified images that will soon emerge on the screen. The camera that was following Kewal is now awaiting him inside the theatre. He pushes through the heavy door, looking up in amazement at the larger-than-life props, such as giant sheets of crisscrossing curtain, backdrop paintings and sculpture. The long shot of the theatrical space that follows gives the full impact of this other (make-belief, magical) world and the large unruly curtains that make several V shapes across the screen are in contrast to the geometric shapes of buildings of the streets—V shapes in black and white cinema are used for distinct dramatic impact as will also be discussed in the chapter on films directed by Guru Dutt.

In Kewal's theatrical world, height and space dwarf the figure on the stage/screen by the sheer vertical scale of props, even as he struggles to make space for himself in the lower centre of the screen (Fig. 6). The lighting catches the fabric fitfully, as also the large classical statue of a human figure in a circle of light at the left edge of the screen, rendering the scene dream- and shadow-like. His eye looks upward in awe but he is also nervously excited in this new space—the viewer is cued by his glance at the enormity of scale, continuous with those forbidding street-side images of the grandeur of the church and opera house. The complete absence of background 'mood' music heightens visual tension. The vertiginous silence is interrupted only when Kewal almost knocks a few props as he walks in the dark—he manages to catch them before they fall, rendering him again a simpleton before such darkly illumined mystery.

Fig. 6 *Source NFAI*

Kewal's point of view from the stage is a wide-angle shot of empty audience seats—a viewing space much larger than anything that the plays of the film (school, street and college drama) have thus far evoked. His past is rendered amateur and even his ambition (for which his father had chastised him) is suddenly felt as paltry. More significantly, the empty seats of the theatre are now occupied by us, the proxy cinematic audience. It is 'the bottomless empathy enhanced by darkness, distance, solitude-in-a-crowd, and regressive, cushioned comfort of a proscenium theatre'.[6] This meta-moment cajoles the viewer into realising the visual privilege and intrusion that she is privy to in this space of action and motivation.

Kewal is shot as a small figure in comparison to the scale of the frame—but he slowly begins to show more confidence in inhabiting that space. He sits down at the centre where the lines of two curtains meet and draws our attention to a moment of anointment, his hands on his knees, unwilling to let the scale intimidate him even though he remains visually dwarfed. The scene cuts to a mid shot of Kewal, a moment of him gathering power and letting his emotions spill over in a surveying glance. There are the characteristic mixed Raj Kapoor expressions—joy and awe, hunger and unkemptness from being on the streets, an overall self-aware self-deprecation. But this shot reveals him as back in possession of the frame—he will now dominate or caress it. He notices a flute on the floor (and flute music begins to play even as he picks it up)—the camera tilts down to his glance and follows his hand as it brings the flute to his face. This act of gently picking up the flute seems to release some of the misery and uncertainty of Kewal's wandering and hungry days. He kisses it and the familiar voice begins speaking—'And what if you lose yourself on the way as you search for your destination?' Kewal recognises it as the voice of his father, shakes his head, his lips unmoving and repeats an old answer—'I will again try to find my way, father.' Both the character and the viewers are reminded of the time the father had asked him to leave the house and he had loudly thanked him for granting him this unburdened and unguilty freedom. As Kewal remembers those words, the vacant theatre-space now no longer intimidates, even though the voices of his father and mother filled his ears from all corners, causing him to sink back into vulnerability. The peremptory questioning of his father and the pleading tone of his mother are distorted in the proscenium which is a mystery space full of unsuspected and obscure aural depths, large classical statues, half-pillars and lamp posts, erratic and serrated lighting. The use of such lighting and props, especially when they simply lie inert and are not absorbed in some theatre scene, serve cinematically as expressing his psyche, with its intermixture of memory, desire and ambition.

In response to the censuring voice of his father (playing in his head) Kewal says rather melodramatically—'I don't like easy pathways. I like twisted pathways filled with thorns.' In this moment, both stage and cinema seem to agree that it is a moment to stand by the distraught character, to applaud not just his difficult rebellion, but to fully acknowledge the dramatic potential of that moment of creativity for both mediums. As Kewal delivers his lines, the stage comes alive to the aural effect of applause (even as the chairs are empty) and in perfect empathy, the spotlights turn on one by one (a ghostly crew seems to be at work), till the stage is fully illumined—it would seem that struggle is the true backstory of theatre. This reconfiguration of stage lighting in the middle of the shot is not a self-conscious interplay of stagecraft and performance but a gesture to cinema, for it is the 'abrupt shifts in tone [that] make us conscious of watching a film'.[7] The sound of applause continues with three quick shots of the empty, dimly lit auditorium chairs from different angles. Even before Kewal becomes a theatre director, before he puts up an actual production in front of a live audience, this moment of self-recognition of his strengths and weakness is a finale and suggests to the viewer that the elaborate paraphernalia on the stage is to facilitate, even stand in, for the character's psychic scape and aspiration.

Kewal launches into a soliloquy, holding forth about theatre but lit and shot as cinema through the use of long and mid shots, background strings and tracking. Now we are indeed presented with him towering over the proscenium stage as if we are in the front row. Low angle shots retain the proscenium effect but there are also close-ups which the proscenium cannot accomplish. What Kewal utters are now new lines, addressed to viewers frontally and in a traditional theatrical, declamatory tone—the cinema coincides with theatre at this heightened moment of direct address. He begins to speak—and it is the generic speech of the artist, of every city that has lakhs of aspiring actors like him. They wish to make their future but are not allowed to. Now it is the public speaker's voice and gesture. As Kewal laments being a social misfit, there are paeans to his loving mother—and yet he cannot help leaving her world, even if what he is leaving is the claustrophobia of the house rather than the mother herself.

The apology to the mother is also a warning to his father that he will make theatre respectable. The triangle of the father (contempt, sarcasm), mother (kindness, pleading) and his own aspiration are delivered with tears and sobs, his body swaying, leaning in and out. The camera frames Kapoor in a manner that emphasises the performance space—a youthful figure in the foreground, striking props, dramatic and troubled gestures. The chairs of the theatre continue to listen silently, empathetically, till Kewal finishes his speech and just when it feels like the emotional pitch of the scene has been saturated, even over-done, all lights turn off, except for two spotlights that continue to make the V that directs our eye to the central figure of the distraught hero (Fig. 7). This becomes the denouement of this impromptu autobiographical play.

Fig. 7 *Source NFAI*

It is time for curtain call. We hear the sound of a single person's clap, more immediate than the earlier (imagined) collective applause. A figure enters, saying 'Wonderful! Truly wonderful'. The figure turns out to be the patron of the theatre, Rajan (who is a painter and thus a visual artist to complement Kewal's kinesthetic creativity). Kewal realises he had an audience after all, one that would help him realise his dream. The theatre is revealed as gift and mystery, the stage as a vast space where one is almost enjoined to ask existential questions. Constantin Stanislavski describes the viscerality of such a moment:

> What excited me was not my lines, not the meaning of what transpired, for the one-actor was devoid of all meanings; what thrilled me was artistic action, playing before spectators. I was excited by the public, by the publicity of my appearance, by the consciousness of the crowd and of myself onshow before it [...] I was excited by the madness of the tempo and the rhythm within me [...] Words and gestures flew out with the rapidity of lightning.[8]

Acting is a sanctioned nakedness and the spontaneous applause of the patron or audience the only true validation that one can hope to find.

The Last Flicker

In the climactic scene of the film, the fire returns in full blaze. Kewal is now a director, with the painter-patron (Rajan) who has given him a theatre, funding and artistic freedom. He has also discovered a new actor whom he puts much faith in—she is a Partition refugee (this is a rare reference to external, sociopolitical history in the film) and the trauma of the event is used by Kewal to forge her in his imagination. He names her Nimmi (the character is played by Nargis). She seems to possess (even though she cannot fully understand it herself) that ineffable quality that Kewal wants—even though Kewal cannot explicitly articulate what he wants. He is on the verge of making peace with his parents—he invites them for the premiere of his show in what is now called Kewal Theatres. So, finally, after all the aborted plays, there is going to be a real play—and this is going to be the last, climactic scene of his past, before which the circle will return to the wedding night. Unlike Kewal's boyhood, the audience this time is milling, walking, coming by car and honking impatiently, there is festivity and hanging illumination outside the theatre—he is a star even before the play begins. The theatre can absorb both the working-class world as well as the limousine-chauffeured one. The scenes of the crowd in theatres are important in this book. Later chapters (especially on Guru Dutt) discuss this double-edged figure of the crowd—the crowd as a motor that can so easily create and destroy, laud and decry. It is also historical—the crowd in the theatre was the only judge in the age before television or the multiplex or the internet. Needless to say, the metafiction of stage and screen continues as the play that Kewal is staging is itself titled *Aag*.

To return to the excitement of Kewal's premiere: the images seamlessly encompass the crowd all the way to the internal world of the proscenium. A decorated earthen pot swings in the air against a black background, followed by a shot of palms playing instruments. Only the hands of the musicians are visible and the instruments seem to float in the middle of the frame—this moment belonging more to the cinematic (that can do visual manipulations) than of the real-time, real-eye performance on the stage that the audience has now settled to watch. Kewal's parents are the sole occupants of a box seat, the mother leaning forward, the father appearing more restrained, sitting farther back. The audience below is rapt—the line that separates the proscenium from the audience is not demarcated as the scene cuts easily from a shot of the audience to a close-up of a generic, silhouetted singer (a recurring trope in R.K. Films) singing of youth and desire, and then to other silhouetted women, their tapping, anklet-laced feet and wrists with bangles tracing graceful gestures. These are bodies not yet filled with meaning. But beyond the group of women, there is one differentiated woman on the parapet of a bridge, tugging and playing with a low lying, flowered branch. This is Nimmi—she is directly lit, the sole occupant of the frame. She emerges as a distinct, single female voice (the playback artist is Shamshad Begum) even as the voice harmonises with the singing of the group. The camera moves towards her with every intercut of the group till there is a close-up, before pulling back again at the end. It is a conventionally lyric-rural setting, hardly the impassioned, unique scene that one imagined Kewal to direct (after all, the talk of needing inner passion, not external beauty that he had earlier instructed Nimmi to achieve). The audience cheers and the curtains close from the sides. At this, we have our first long (and wide) shot of the inside of the theatre—a top angle view from behind the audience. It is time for the intermission. The proscenium arch is a centred enticing curve, the curtains diaphanous, like an eye with its lid closed (Fig. 8). This is a delayed establishing shot of the theatre interiors and signals forthcoming narrative gravitas.

Fig. 8 *Source NFAI*

One is now moved into a different, fuzzier frame—though the action is within the play (as the play is only at half-time), the dramatic events will henceforth happen outside. The true theatre, as has happened throughout the film, seems to find its centre of action outside the proscenium. The play has thus far revealed little of Kewal's claim to genius—but events of the world outside will now take over, returning to our theme of drama (and fire) being unable to keep to its boundaries. The audience itself becomes redundant—as unindividuated as the rural scene inside the play and only there to applaud or confirm and later, to panic and run. The drama will take place between Kewal, the painter-patron Rajan, Nimmi and, to a smaller extent, the parents. Kewal and Nimmi are happy—though he says, understatedly, that her performance needed even more submergence in the character. She is impatient, keener on an expected declaration of love but he is too absorbed in the play. He also seeks out his mother in this moment of pride and achievement. She is weeping tears of joy. He seeks her blessing—but she seems less interested in the play and instead begs for a daughter-in-law. While for him the play is about theatre, for Nimmi it is a way to find love and for his mother, the success of theatre is about bringing him back into a domestic fold. He leaves in annoyance as neither woman seems interested in his play for its own sake. It makes sense that he then seeks his friend Rajan who had previously agreed that art can be its own end. But that conversation does not go well for his friend confesses love for the same woman (Nimmi). The film studio (as is the theatre) is already a dream-space; so much emotional drama happens, not just on the proscenium stage but everywhere around—the audience-spaces, the green room, the painting studio of Rajan located above. Drama flows everywhere and the official stage cannot contain it—soon, it will be the fire that flows everywhere. The only certainty for the artist is that the show must go on and that the play has to resume after this passion-filled intermission.

We return to the proscenium and its timeless rural world (as depicted on stage) but the affective centre has now shifted to the personal lives of the patron, star and director. While the play unfolds, Kewal storms into Nimmi's dressing room, asking if it was true that she desired him. The long conversation where Kewal tries to convince Nimmi to love another is significant for giving her the space to explain her attraction to Kewal—the reason, she tells him, is his beautiful looks, his blue eyes, his fair hair (all that he rued in the first scene of the film). A stagehand interrupts, telling her that it is time for her to get back on stage. On the stage, an actor is telling the hero to risk his life for his country: the plot of the play seems bathetic now, compared to the drama taking place beyond the proscenium. In contrast to the conventionality of the play-set (the rural groupings carrying their torches, the bridge, the tree under which the lover waits), there is greater theatricality (and more deft lighting) in the shots of Kewal as he stands offstage with props casting dark shadows, all indicating the topography of a tortured psyche.

Nimmi mouths lines on stage that repeat her recent conversation with Kewal—she is helpless in love. Her lover (in the play) has gone to war and even as the play continues, the intercuts in the scene break any last vestiges of exclusive stage space. While Nimmi bends low on the wooden frame of a bridge on the stage and looks out to the left of the frame the reaction shot is of an emotionally agitated Kewal standing in the wings looking to the right of the frame—the world of inside and outside the play is entirely blurred and their gazes cut across the theatre/real-world divide. The song talks of being looted by fate with even the eyes having no tears left. It is sung unexpectedly slowly, the lips moving softly, Nimmi raising her body in tune with the tempo of the song. The music only shifts when the shot returns to Kewal in close-up, teary-eyed, more overtly emotional than Nimmi. It is now his turn to be emotionally naked, bereft of the pure ascetic pursuit of Art. There is an accusation in the lyrics of the song ('Why did you make me yours and then leave me?'), and this is confirmed by a close-up of Kewal shedding tears against a pillar. The intercuts now alternate between him and all that he holds dear—Nimmi, his parents, the audience, the crew and actors preparing torches for the next scene of the play.

It is a moment asking for a fatal act. Kewal suddenly takes a torch from the stagehand—a burning stick in the dark. As the song continues on stage, the flames come ever closer to Kewal's face, overwhelming the screen, swallowing up his face (Fig. 10). The viewer realises the horror of what is happening in five quick shots—Kewal has burnt his own face. The sequence of fire and face establishes a final continuity between theatre and film and how both are reimagined (via a literal 'trial by fire') by cinematic technique.

Fig. 9 *Source NFAI*

As Kewal falls out of the frame, the torch falls onto the flammable grass on the stage. The growing fire does take a while to register on everyone assembled: Nimmi continues singing and the parents and audience continue watching. She is singing, 'You have just left me as a tale [*afsana*] for the world'—a plaything to art. But now the fire is blazing and the first to notice are the stagehands who begin to run—this is even as the singing voice does not let up. It is only the scream of the mother that signals the conflagration to the entire audience. The properties on stage are now all ablaze and the audience is both running away as well as running towards it to quench the fire with buckets of water. Several people are on the stage amidst the giant falling curtains and attempting to douse the fire—such an action

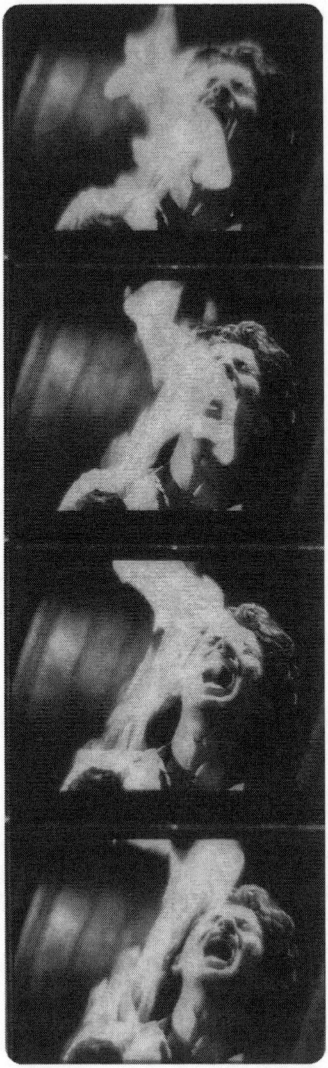

Fig. 10 Source NFAI

again breaches the fourth wall of the proscenium play. There is a wildness to the fire that lights faces unpredictably, leaving in its wake snaking shadows. Everyone is shouting '*aag*'—a word that now signifies the fire in the theatre, the name of the play being staged and the film that the viewer is watching. The repeated shots of the proscenium arch with fire on both sides perfectly signal this semantic fusion. Amidst all the mayhem there emerges a fleeting dissolve of Kewal's burning, screaming face, the artist burning with/for his work, his passion (Fig. 10).

The signboard of Kewal Theatres is afire; a chapter of vanity has been destroyed. After the roar of the fire, there is hushed silence—the next shot is of the audience, now composed, waiting to see if Kewal will emerge alive out of the blaze. The viewing has shifted from inside the theatre to the outdoor—there can be no spectacle without an audience. The only recognisable faces in the anonymous audience are Nimmi and the father (the mother seems to have disappeared)—again, this is the offstage play, the true site of tension and heroism. All eyes are on the entrance of the theatre that is shaped exactly like the proscenium arch of the stage that has just burnt down—it is now visually alive with the fire and smoke within. Finally, in a long shot, a monumentalised, silhouetted figure emerges in the open doorway, with his arms at his sides (Fig. 11). The camera keeps cutting from the expectation in the audience to the unmoving man shaped like a smouldering tree trunk in a dying fire. It is Nimmi who rushes to him—but she screams when she gets to him (a scream that mimics the wedding-night scream of the opening sequence). Here too, the fingers cover the mouth and she screams repeatedly through the shots that follow.

Fig. 11 *Source NFAI*

The light catches Kewal's unburnt side as he asks Nimmi to come closer but she is repulsed and moves back—the viewer grasps the horror through her reaction. A long shot follows, his burnt figure visible but only from a distance—there is no fully lit close-up. He mocks her earlier comments on his beauty. He says that beauty is not everything. His face has been symmetrically burnt as if to prove that both face and soul (*surat* and *seerat*) need to complement each other—the theatricality of this scene is reminiscent of his monologue in the empty theatre which Rajan had applauded and which had launched his career. This is to be his last staging and performance. After delivering his lines, Kewal collapses.

From this heightened pitch, the film has to modulate itself towards resolution. The scene shifts to the hospital where Kewal's face is covered by a bandage. Nimmi visits him and as Kewal touches her hand he realises that she has a ring—she is betrothed to Rajan. The *Shakuntala* theme of (mis)recognition continues. This is the end of the film's long flashback, and the shot dissolves back to the first scene of Kewal at the window, the unburned profile again lit, wishing all his former, fruitless loves well. And then, of course, follows the happy, true recognition that the woman he is married to is the Nimmi of his childhood—she had simply changed her name to Sudha. The circle is closed, the marriage consummated. The last visual of the film, the one that celebrates this fusing of two minds and bodies, does not stay in the nuptial chamber but returns to the theatrical comfort of the prosceniumesque framing—this time, the window frame mimics it for the viewer. The rebellious image (of cinema) finds its full expression by circumvention and stylistically reframing.

Aag was not particularly commercially successful and what made Raj Kapoor famous was his next production, *Barsaat* (Rain, 1949). However, it is in *Aag* that we see experimentation with a visual lexicon that communicates the protagonist's seething passion. In many films that Kapoor made after this, the image tends to settle into serving the storyline (either of thwarted or realised passion) and we see less of the deliberate and intuitive play of visual lyricism. Innovative visual lyricism paves way for the plot (in *Aag*) rather than the other way round in his later films. The displaced proscenium arch, however, recurs in *Barsaat*, especially in the pillars and frames of the lake-house on stilts that the protagonist rents in idyllic Kashmir. In *Barsaat*, Raj Kapoor takes on the persona of Pran, a young man from the city, and his lady love is again played by Nargis—she is the daughter of the caretaker of the house. This structure is a studio space designed to replicate the monumentality and verticality of a theatre set with its two levels, a distinct (watery) foreground, clear entry/exit points for the character as well as constant ascent and descent. The protagonist is often shown playing his beloved violin on the balcony of this house that again evokes a theatrical balcony, while the ornate tall pillars, gently sloping roof and low wooden banisters in the foreground invite us into a proscenium space. Most of the significant meetings between the lovers happen here—it functions almost as a Shakespearean balcony where lovers divided by class and family find temporary reprieve and solace. In a highly sexualised scene where his lover steals to him in the middle of the night drawn by the crescendos and diminuendos of the tides of his music, Pran's violin is knocked out of his hands as she rushes to take its place. The proscenium arch is breached as the camera moves close to the lovers. Her body twists, turns and writhes in an absolute entanglement of bodies. The shots are from the top angle (the fiddle appearing phallic). He says that he wants to play her like a violin till she quivers from head to toe ('*Ji chahata hai tumhare dil ke taaron ko is tarah ched doon ke bas sar se paavn tak jhanjhana utho*'; Fig. 12). She confesses that such has already happened but he has not heard its sound. He indicates that playing the violin has become an outlet for his (unmet) sexual needs, his fingers bloodied from so much playing. She puts her open lips to his fingers as the sexual tension continues to rise (Fig. 13). This scene had started with the full-frontal proscenium framing of the balcony setting. But after the loss of the violin and the close proximity of bodies, the scene sculpts new emotive sites (the close-up of lip on finger, distorted angles of vision) for the camera to enter and occupy. The shift from the proscenium to the cinematic is indexed by the viewer's new intimacy with the sexual—the eye can travel in cinema in a manner that generates a new oeuvre of sexual imagery.

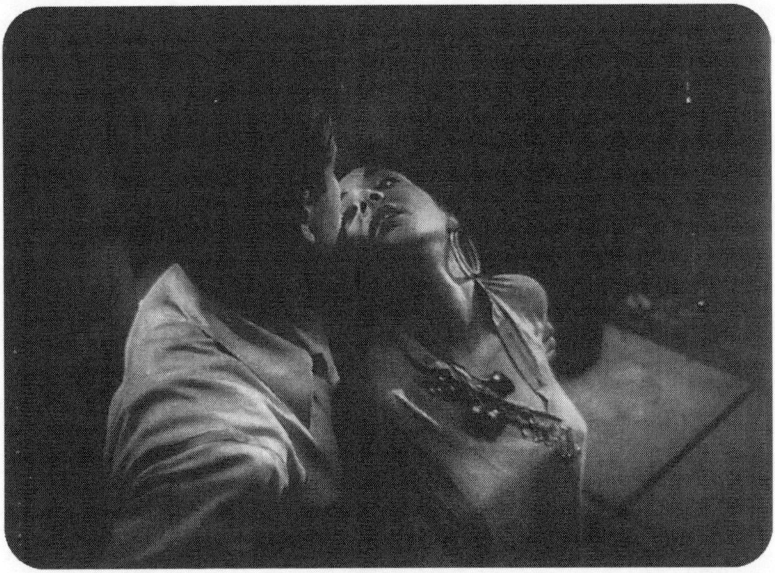

Fig. 12 *Source NFAI*

Fig. 13 *Source NFAI*

Till this scene of man-woman-balcony-violin, we were only offered the purity of the woman's sexual passion—there had been no backstory, only a threadbare parental commentary (for her, not for him). Indeed, neither of them gave any rationale for their love beyond their submergence in the moment and the representation of passion and sexual love in a 'frozen' image in this 1949 film is unique in Indian cinema. That Raj Kapoor—who has been seen as trying 'to purvey the image of the one-man industry'[9]—was aware of the import of this moment can be assumed from his choosing to make an icon of this moment to represent his production house R.K. Films. The real-life couple (Kapoor and Nargis) who 'epitomized a modern freedom and lack of inhibition',[10] and were 'indicative of some of the changes in conceptualizing scandal, gossip and the private'[11] reinforced that extra-filmic commentary, with representations on-screen that carved a new visual language of not just aspirational desire but sexual compatibility and fulfillment.

In his very next directorial offering, *Awaara* the same scene is evoked in the logo of the opening credits through the recognisable figurines of Raj Kapoor and Nargis—the knocked-out violin has been restored in his hands, she is draped over his right hand and our perspective has moved from the top angle to a low angle of the two standing over the letters R and K. The icon is further modified to lose recognisable features and become more geometric in *Shree 420*—this time with a dramatic sky (clouds and beaming rays of light) forming the background. Perhaps there is some inkling of the impending personal and professional parting between Kapoor and Nargis not so long after the release of this film or perhaps the director is now aware that the roles he has created of lovers on screen have become representative of a generation—here representation means generic and anonymous, an iconography no longer associated with specific star faces.

However, faces continue to be a particular fixation with Raj Kapoor—in *Mera Naam Joker* (My Name is Joker, 1970), the film that Raj Kapoor considered his directorial masterpiece and most autobiographical film, the protagonist is a professional circus clown. The film did not live up to his expectations in the box office and Raj Kapoor never acted again in his directorial ventures—what is of interest, however, is that an acting-directing career that started with an obsession with the face as burnt, ends with the face hidden behind the thick parodic makeup of the clown. The more telling example of this ongoing fixation is a still later directorial venture: *Satyam Shivam Sundaram* (Truth, God, Beauty, 1978), which is a return to *Aag* in its central premise. The film is about a character with a face that is half-burnt, exactly like Kewal of *Aag*—this time it is the right profile of a beautiful woman whose relationship with her shallow lover (he cares only for physical beauty) is possible only by splitting her into two personas—the burnt profile identified with the wife and the unburnt profile with the lover.

Raj Kapoor may be unique in how he places face and body at the centre of the image-making process with both constantly spilling out of the frame. Nothing quite matters as much as the movement of the body and the face of the actor. This is not just narcissism—it may be that too—but it is also a singular initiation, a distinct and vantage starting-point, for the image-repertoire that Hindi cinema is. The burnt/painted face is a doubled, shadowed face that forces the aesthetic (and the audience) to new extremities, especially of the image of passion—there has not quite been an emblem of romance as the Raj Kapoor–Nargis coupling. For them, the viewer embraces many perspectives of distortion, scarring, masking—the star's face is the primary mode of the amplification of vision and affect. In contrast, as shown in the next chapter on Nutan (and Bimal Roy), amplification will depend less on the face of the star and more on the idea of restraint, performance and the submergence of the imagination of 'character' to meticulous visual design, one that seeks to more organically integrate the synthesised elements of pacing, setting, motif, theme and performance.

Female (Self) Portraiture in Monochrome: Nutan in Bimal Roy's *Sujata* (1959) and *Bandini* (1963)

'Performance means: never for the first time; it means: for the second to the nth time. Reflexive means to see the self in the self-and-other.'

—Richard Schechner[1]

In a visual echo of its title, the 1963 film *Bandini* (Female Prisoner) starts with new arrivals to prison, as seen in the quick sequence of images—the dust and smoke of a vehicle, the prison official receiving a file with details of the newcomers, the customary name-calling of prisoners as they enter. The official stands against the vertical lines of the prison gate and in front of him are a huddle of women covered in blankets: with nothing to distinguish one from another, they are an anonymous collectivity. Each time he calls a name, he looks up and no response is heard—it is implied from the non-verbal reaction of the first name called in the establishing shot that the correct response is to step forward in silence and with downcast eyes. Kalyani is the third name to be called—the official's eyes again rise from his file. We catch our first glimpse of the protagonist—a mid-close shot of the prisoner Kalyani played by the actress Nutan (Fig. 1A). The camera's affinity to this face is unmistakable. The central composition, the modulated light, the drapes of the blanket cocooning her face, the margin in the frame for her swiftly raised head; her irate stare at the official (Fig. 1B). In response, the official quickly lowers his eyes. In this quick and simple back and forth of shots, the situation and personality of the character is not only quickly established but the viewer is also being prepared for a unique dynamic between performance and cinematic frame. As is to be expected from cinema, the actor is performing within a given frame but is also as an active agent and participant in the process of image-making.

Fig. 1A *Source NFAI*

Fig. 1B *Source NFAI*

Andre Bazin writes about the shifting relevance of the actor from theatre to cinema—in theatre, he points to 'the reciprocal awareness of the presence of audience and actor' which happens through performance but with cinema, the actor risks becoming 'an accessory, like an extra' in relation to the décor, one of the many elements that create a cinematic spectacle.[2] This transition and linkage between theatre and cinema are evident in Raj Kapoor's work—as discussed, we have seen how he 'imported' the large world of theatre into the cinematic frame (the physical site of the proscenium, the amplified acting style). However, Bazin has rightly cautioned us against this importation—each visual element and performative style has to be transformed and acting has to reinvent itself to distinguish itself from the profusion of decor. How is the performance to be contra-distinguished from the diverse mélange of cinematic elements in terms of both presentation on the side of the actor and director and in terms of the reception by a viewer? We locate this question in the professional collaboration of director Bimal Roy (1909–1966) and the actor Nutan (1936–1991). Indeed, this concern may well be the hallmark of Bimal Roy's auteurship. Roy, who has already made his presence in this book as the editor of *Mahal*, had one of the most illustrious directorial careers in Hindi cinema and to date is the winner of the maximum number of 'Best Director' awards. His legacy is substantial and as pointed out by the film scholar M.K. Raghavendra, several influential film-makers of the 1950s and 1960s worked with him—Hrishikesh Mukherjee, Gulzar, Basu Bhattacharya and Basu Chatterjee.[3] Though Roy's visual aesthetic has been widely applauded, there is little scholarship on the precise elements of the visual quality of his work as well as of the relation of that visuality to performance.

Roy responds to Bazin's conundrum thus: he renders the excessiveness of props 'invisible' or allegorical in nature (bare walls, prison bars, shadows). In other words, the chief manner of restoring the actor's centrality is by keeping the props to a minimum, both in terms of the horizontality of the frame as well as its depth. This economy and passivity of props/images allow the performance and its affective correlate to etch and grow itself. As Deleuze reminds us,

> affects are not individuated like people or things, but nevertheless they do not blend into the indifference of the world. They have singularities which enter into virtual conjunction and each time

> constitute a complex entity. It is like points of melting, or of boiling, or condensation, of coagulation, etc. That is why faces which express various affects, or the various points of the same affect, do not merge into a single [affect] which would obliterate them.[4]

The first shot of Kalyani's face and demeanor represents this distinctly visualised and embodied biography—in line with Deleuze, her face captures the fleetingness of the many affects without merging or obliterating their differences.

This chapter studies the mutuality between performance and visual technique in two films directed by Bimal Roy with Nutan, as protagonist—*Sujata* (1959) and *Bandini* (1963). To better contextualise her performance register, the chapter will begin with a brief analysis of an earlier film *Seema* (Limit/Horizon, 1955), the one that established her as a formidable actor—she was barely twenty years old. The films interpret the evolution of Nutan's inimitable style—as an angry, wronged woman in *Seema*, as a social outcaste in *Sujata* (1959) to culminate in the evocativeness of the impassioned figure of a woman convicted of murder in *Bandini* (1963). All three narratives studied here—*Seema*, *Sujata* and *Bandini*—embody marginal characters: an orphan, a Dalit and a prisoner, respectively. They inhabit interstitial spaces—the rehabilitation *ashram*, the kitchen, the prison—all highly unusual roles for a leading actor in commercial cinema. Ravi Vasudevan attributes this

> deployment of a star discourse to make such explorations [subalternity] more palatable. Thus the casting of Nutan, the impeccable high-caste actress, daughter of Shobhana Samarth, the Sita of Vijay Bhat's *Ramayana* (1946), probably affords the spectator a reassuring distance from the social referent of these films.[5]

However, what this chapter is interested in is less the social referent and more the achieved reciprocity of the visual and the performative in these selections from Nutan's filmography. Whereas in *Seema* there is rather the simple and not inaccurate givenness of the exploitation of the labour and beauty of a young woman, in *Bandini* there is a superior, more muted sense of sorrow. In the latter, the superiority of Bimal Roy's film-making (especially lighting and editing) allows a more evocative unfolding of difficult, 'un-womanly' affects, such as rage and isolation. The achievement is particularly haunting with Nutan—here was an actor who could represent sheer joy, lips dancing either lightly over the words of a song or alternatively, show the ripple of the muscle-line on her throat as she sings. Few actors have used bodies or stances or facial expressions better—especially with regard to both joy as well as a sense of hurt and injustice within the diegetic space of the film.

It may indeed be argued that acting begins when the prioritised fixation of the camera with the star is broken. Ironically, when the actor is chiefly a star, the more likely she is in real terms a prop—of the level of a beautiful landscape or a plush interior. For the star, what gets prioritised is an ever-mobiliseable paraphernalia—the flattering camera angle that masks the double chin or that highlights the line of the strong male jaw. In contrast to the star, the actor must seek to appear in a more naked light, be more individuated in gesture and affect, and must compete within the shot with the other elements that also become increasingly visible with the turning-down of star power—these elements include music, editing and pacing, the entirety of unique *mise en scène*. Beyond the figure of the star, other visibilities emerge—including the silences, visual abstraction and blankness (walls, bars, screens, partitions and shadows) distinctive to Bimal Roy. Acting is at its strongest when it conveys beyond verbalisation or plot—the body moves at its own register of the representations of pain and affect. In inhabiting such roles, Nutan greatly expanded the repertoire of the female actor star in the performative and visual idiom of the 1950s and 1960s—the chapter demonstrates this accomplishment. As this chapter foregrounds performance, when the reference is specifically to the performative repertoire, the name of the actor

(Nutan) is used and when the reference is to plot or character, the name of the relevant protagonist (Gauri, Sujata or Kalyani) of the film is employed.

The Alienated Domestic

In his memoir, actor Naseeruddin Shah writes of the female stars he had watched on screen: 'And there were the luminous ladies: Waheeda Rehman and Nargis, still Hindi cinema's most modern actresses; the divinely gorgeous Madhubala, the statuesque Meena Kumari, the unbearably sexy and utterly unattainable Nutan, the off-centre Tanuja'.[6] The adjectival emphasis on sexuality that is unattainable bears scrutiny. For the puzzlement is that Nutan's impact rested less on the explicit glamour of a Madhubala and more on roles that are far more in engagement with the domestic, even if it is the domestic that she is continually falling out of or unable to return to. From *Seema* one can see an enduring trope—the woman who at one level wishes to be nothing more than a loved daughter or wife but is yet someone who on being denied, thus, conjures up a credible, spontaneous rage, a rage that speaks to larger, disenfranchised womanhood.

Directed by Amiya Chakrabarty and cinematographed by V. Babasaheb, *Seema* is the story of Gauri (played by Nutan), an orphan living amidst the working-class settlements of Bombay. She is routinely ill-treated by her uncle and his wife. At work, she is wrongly accused of theft. This leads to her being put in an orphanage (*anaath ashram*), run by a reform-minded manager Ashok (played by noted actor Balraj Sahni). By this time, after the piling up of a lifetime of injustice, Gauri has begun to react violently to people—her uncle and aunt, the police and even the helpful employees of the *ashram*. At one point she breaks windows and furniture and beats up the thief who falsely got her into the *ashram*. While the moral strand of the narrative is that of reforming her anger, the achievement of Nutan is to perform against the grain of such paternalist reform that continually sought to co-opt her into the roles of dutiful daughter, and—after the expected, inevitable romance with Ashok—the romantic partner. When one speaks of the 'domestic' in the context of this film, one does not mean just the physical space of the tenement or *ashram* but the moral tissue that constantly seeks to bring her back to the normative roles of the sweet-tempered daughter/help/caregiver. Irrespective of where she is (the tenement or the *ashram*), the 'domestic' functions as this semiotic cluster that seeks to irrevocably draw her back to the sisterly care of the younger women in the *ashram*, even as she continually adjusts and accommodates. This is of course what Ashok's benign personality ultimately signifies. What this analysis instead seeks to achieve is to read Nutan's performance as an exemplified alienation against the familiar domestic/courtship trope of the 'taming of the shrew'.

The credits of the film start with a long shot of a lone figure in a steady purposive stride along the line of the horizon at the lower edge of the screen—it is established from the beginning that this is a woman fighting fate alone and with courage. After this defiant, allegorical, solitary stride, the film begins with the protagonist entrenched in a typically oppressive family situation. Her first appearance on the screen is unobtrusive, her back to the camera, her hair hiding her face, sitting bent on the kitchen floor making rotis in a posture of impoverished drudgery. It was not the commonest sight in a commercial film to have the lead female introduced on-screen with everyday housework. The adoptive parents are scolding her for lax domestic work. The small, rectangular window on the mud wall has prison-like bars (the connection of Nutan and bars is an enduring image—it is explored more fully in the last section of this chapter, in the film *Bandini* where she is a prisoner). In *Seema*, Gauri's body amidst hastened, unending physical domestic labour still radiates youthful force even as other aspects signal docility (the voice, the face humbly turned away as it is scolded). The body conveys both pliancy as well as a repressed yet emerging resistance—and the latter is best represented by the pace of movement, the pained shutting of eyes or the strength of her gaze, by her standing still even as she does not reply to the words and physical jabs of the aunt.

The embodiment of affect is built up slowly. There is the flinching as of a startled deer, as well as a low-voiced explanation for why she had not yet finished the cooking. The breathing (and Nutan is adept at using breath to signal a sense of injustice even when silent) replicates this mixture of docility and defiance. When the latter trait of defiance begins to dominate the movie, the transformation is rendered more credible by this older muscle and posture memory. Gauri carries this stance and body even into her workplace—a parallel domestic world where she has again been hired to do menial labour and where the scolding and harassment remain continuous with the home. Entering this space, Gauri quickly tucks her sari, adjusts her bangles and sits on her haunches easily and forcefully. The later transformation of character (into hostility and violence) takes place as anger directed at both sites/institutions—the family and the workplace. The anger matures only in the third site of the *ashram* which has elements of both home and workplace, albeit now in a new environment where she does not have to work or serve and where all the attention is directed at someone (the eventual love interest) who functions both as the good father and the good employer.

It is rare for even contemporary Indian films to represent constant male harassment that women domestic help have to endure—*Seema* also exposes all the minute differences in the hierarchy of domestic help, male servant, etc. The body language of Gauri's defiance is also stronger vis-à-vis the injustice of harassment by, on the one hand, the male co-worker and, on the other hand, by her family—she is more helpless regarding the latter. The male co-worker both harasses her as well as constantly threatens to expose her to the police—the mistress also easily evokes the police and indeed Gauri is soon wrongly picked up for theft. Criminalisation is a reality that the poor can easily slip into. To add to this, there is the sense of her bringing ill-luck and inauspiciousness for she was an adopted orphan. *Seema* was prescient in its characterisation of the 'angry young' protagonist. This is long before Amitabh Bachchan and contemporary indeed to the 'angry young men' of the British literary world or the moral capital of the rage of the actor Nargis in *Mother India* (made a little later in 1957 and which had all the idealised weight of motherhood and the single-woman rural labourer). *Seema* does not have the simple linearity of rage and the taming of that rage—rather there are tamings but then there are also returns to that rage, each cycle of rage expressed differently (throwing furniture, tearing pillows and playing with the cotton-stuffing, smashing windows, breaking plates, locking herself in—there is a certain joyous expressive defiance). Yet, like *Mother India*, the film has to take pains to justify and explain female anger.

It is evident that the protagonist in *Seema* cannot easily claim anger, even though this anger is of a genuinely disadvantaged and oppressed woman. The anger cannot also be represented by just facial movements or vocalisms or even as a monologue—it would seem too scripted and lacking in spontaneity. Nutan's acting improves on the mere plot-trait of the 'suffering, angry woman' by having the tension and stances of her body convey more than an explicit speech raging against the world's iniquity. There is a seamlessness to the performance, the anger articulated not in isolation but continuous with other related affects, such as desolation, sorrow, guilt. Gauri, falsely arrested for theft, is acquitted by the court but only to be thrown out of her home. Unable to find work because of her police records, destitute and distraught, she starts to walk the streets of the city. Her tall figure can contract, slouch, walk slowly towards the camera: the camera moves above her, especially in scenes when she is defeated and the whole sequence (of navigating the streets of the city) is a long reaction shot, something that Nutan is particularly skilled in and is later used to exemplary effect by Bimal Roy. There are long takes that she sustains with her body—the stiffness, indignation and nervousness stay through several sequences (which depict her being rejected from the house and several types of employment), till it shifts register in response to a song sung by a street-artist. By now, as Gauri herself says, she has nowhere to go in the world. It is in this context that the viewer can see at some length the distinctiveness of Nutan's performance.

During the opening prelude of this song-sequence, Gauri settles down against an unknown wall, defeated by the rejection and judgement of the world. Her face is already akin to a vulnerable wound. She turns her head to listen to street performers (that include singing and dancing children) who seem to be in an equally pitiful state. The camera lingers on her as her eyes respond to the plaintive words of the religious song that pleads for support to the hapless. As is often the case with street performance, a woman throws a coin from her balcony. This coin inadvertently lands at Gauri's feet, and her reaction is immediate and sharp. The viewer is only too aware of how much this coin would mean to the hungry and homeless woman, even as one realises that it would be wrong of her to pick a coin meant for a destitute other. The tension builds in the shots that follow—the heartfelt singing of the performers and the beads of sweat on Gauri's brow as her eyes move from the performers to the coin at her feet. In perfect affinity with her thoughts, the camera tilts up from the clenched toes (besides the coin) to her face and later tilts down from her face to the toes and coin, her rising and lowering eyes providing the cue and rhythm to the shot (Fig. 2A). The lyrics of the song are synchronous to the situation—how one's integrity (*imaan*) wavers when tormented by hunger. An extraordinary moment of bodily emoting follows. The screen is filled by the now-familiar close shot of Gauri's feet and the coin by her toe—she hesitantly pulls back her left foot, just barely, then slowly reaches forward, fully covers the coin with her toes and drags it back—this time, leaving deep anguished groves in the sand (Fig. 2B). The tension of the song is that between its message (it is a religious song), her sense of impropriety at desiring the coin, and her hunger and desperation—all of this is emoted with the propulsive force of her whole body, a vulnerable woman in an unsafe public space. Even the toes seem to throb as she looks fretfully side-to-side to see if anyone is watching. The whole song is a torment with feet and coin—the toes initially hold it hesitantly yet firmly. The coin makes the song less abstract and more real—there is god and money and hunger, and her hunted look is that of an innocent criminal.

Fig. 2A *Source NFAI*

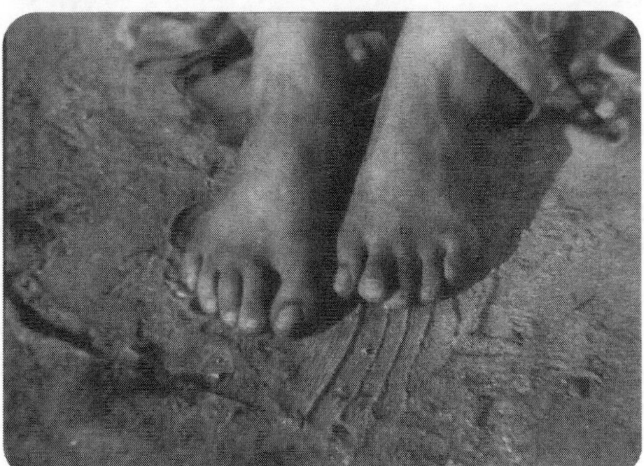

Fig. 2B *Source NFAI*

As the song ends, Gauri sees her harasser, the male domestic help who had falsely accused her. The song has played its alchemy and helped resolve her actions: she returns the coin to the performers and moves towards the man in a warrior pose, elbows extended out, akimbo, stiff and straight-backed—hearing her peremptory voice has already scared the man. There is squatness to her stance, she is heaving, radiating anger, a stout stick hidden behind her gently beating her back in a slow rhythm. Her back and shoulder blades stand out—she is going to enjoy her revenge and she spells out clearly and slowly (and even smilingly) how he had ruined her. The man is soon trapped in a room with nowhere to go (she has secured the door). A little later, she does hit him squarely and fiercely and then again in front of the constable who had come to rearrest her. By now, the rage is everywhere in her body and face, and she maintains this through the police questioning. She remains unapologetic when her uncle and aunt come to the police station—her body has inaugurated a new set of postures and defiant attitudes.

Finally coerced and cajoled to go to the *ashram*, Gauri's body (tall, gracile and wiry) demonstrates its anger by towering over the elder women and peers meant to look after her, by her athleticism in attempts at flight and by her anger directed even against children—her affect overflows frames and sequences. There is no easy movement from rage to pacification. Even as the *ashram* tries many tricks including sentimental religious songs, the viewer for a long time sees a display of a rage rare for a female protagonist in Indian cinema—dropping plates, hitting and fighting with women, face contorted in a feral manner. Indeed, the overall sentimentality of the *ashram* only abets her rage. Despite finding her place and peace among the people and atmosphere of the *ashram*, she is restless to seek revenge against the man who had falsely accused her and manages to leave the premises in the cover of the night, jumping over its tall walls. When she meets the man, she exhausts her rage on him—he falls to the floor and she hits him repeatedly with the stick. The low angle of the camera takes the position of the man being beaten but is still constructed with some empathy for her rage, even as she explodes.

There is growing anxiety in the *ashram* about whether Gauri will return or not—after she seems to have run away. The manager, whose relationship with Gauri has been shown as tender and trusting, is confident that she will. And indeed, Gauri is shown hurrying to the large closed gates of the *ashram*. Just as she reaches the gates, she stops, her back to the camera. It is the familiar stance: hands held away from the body, fingers curled towards palms, the warrior posture (Fig. 3A). The camera slowly tracks towards her as she too starts to slowly step back towards it. We hear a voice-over of her thoughts (in her voice) telling her to escape and enjoy her freedom. When she turns the viewer sees a delirious face, one that is unexpected (Fig. 3B).

Fig. 3A *Source NFAI*

Fig. 3B Source NFAI

The face and body are now tense as a musical string—there is a prospect of freedom and flight on the one hand, and love and duty on the other. This is a marvelous moment in the film—though the male character (waiting inside for the woman to return) has the song—the scene is essentially anchored in her long, tensed reaction shot. If there is a moment when it may be claimed that silence is superior even to song this may be it. Gauri has to emote without using the traditional Hindi film props of song/voice/instrumentation—all these are the background for another sustained track of her reaction. The beginning of the song is this unalloyed long reaction shot, silent, concentrated this time on the face, not body. Indeed the conflict is partially visualised as a conflict between body and face (the body is determined, purposeful, assertive, defiant, oriented towards flight and resistance) but the face (mouth on the verge of tears, darting pupils) is more evidently conflicted. Though the acting of rage is more unique, there also has to be the performance of the descent from the high plateau of that rage. The plot techniques used for this are the traditional ones of romance (Ashok, the benevolent manager of the *ashram*) and song.

Gauri's dilemma between duty and rebellion/freedom is lovingly traced by a camera that tracks with her confused steps. At the final crescendo of his song, the decision is taken and Gauri runs back to re-enter the gates she had resisted up till then.

Returning to the *ashram*, however, does not mean that the rage has been resolved. For the rage had more to do with the collective injustices of her life, something that cannot be erased by beating one man. The anger can only be resolved in the space of love and in the security of the *ashram*. Kept in solitary confinement as punishment, Gauri starts to again play out her frustration—she breaks the window glass, tears pillows, overturns the bed and so on. Ashok allows a full play of her anger, even standing exposed to it—she threatens him directly with a shard of glass.

With time and largely through his persistent goodness, humour, patience and recognition of her singing talent, she changes. Again, Nutan performs with her entire body—at the appropriate plot point it becomes entirely limp and deflated and Ashok has to pull her contrite body to the room with the tanpura. When she sings, Nutan makes her body erect, alert, like Hindustani classical musicians are trained to sit. Lyricist Javed Akhtar quotes Lata Mangeshkar as having picked Nutan as her favourite at lip-synching, the realism of her throat movement during the difficult *taans*[7] of this particular song—*mana mohana bade jhoote.*[8] During and after the song, Nutan's body radiates freshness, sensuality, absorption and finally, contentment. She aligns her spine with the verticality of the tanpura—and shows a new assurance and joy, a new sense of fragility.

In the final sequences, it is revealed that Ashok is very ill. It is now her faith that has to save his life, just as his had earlier redeemed hers. Gauri has to perform the reversal of that initial rage and again, her awareness of the camera and her fellow actors' movements results in her visual transformation from wrathful to nursing. In this new situation of fear and vulnerability, many of the earlier techniques of acting still hold: she has to raise her eye at the right word, has to lean just right into the space of the co-actor. These would be done differently in rage (where there is little awareness of others' space) as opposed to nursing, where there is a hyper consciousness of intimacy and distance. In many films of the era, romance is often indissociable from caretaking—one notices this in many of the films discussed in this book and it will continue to function as a trope. Gauri has to attune her body from rage to Ashok's more compassionate, benign passivity. The actorly challenge is to work the nursing sequence in such a manner that—though the camera's sympathy and foregrounding will prioritise the ill person—Nutan may also discreetly claim the screen. The last minutes are reclamation of the more stoic performance: silence, eyebrows, voices and sighs that dance lightly on her lip. The closing scene where she is running on the seashore, right to left of frame, mirrors the opening shot of her stride across the cloud-weighted horizon. The final top angle which tracks to a close-up that has the two faces filling the frame allows both—the ill and the nurse—to be shot with an egalitarian sympathy, with thus no border (the '*seema*' of the title) between them. They have both alternated the roles of the saviour and the saved and indeed it is she who has ended in the redeemer's role, running powerfully along the seashore actively claiming the frame and the role of the benefactor.

The Still Listener

The career trajectories of director Bimal Roy and Nutan first overlapped when Roy was at the zenith of his career—the critical acclaim of *Do Bigha Zameen* (1953) and the commercial success of *Devdas* (1955) and *Madhumati* (1958) was behind him. The overlap began with the social drama *Sujata* (1959) named after the lead eponymous protagonist played by Nutan and with cinematography by Kamal Bose. Sumita S. Chakravarty points out that '*Sujata*'s theme of stability and change seems to reproduce its maker's own transitional state [...] Its mechanisms of pleasure, blend of realism and idealism and the humanitarian vision that it embodies denote a powerful, if fading, current in the fifties symbolic universe'[9]. Chakravarty offers a skilled and detailed thematic reading of the film, however, the attempt in the present study is to not predicate the reading of the visual on the thematic but rather to see the image-set as a separable aesthetic.

A long childhood sequence precedes Nutan's first appearance on screen. It takes nearly three-quarters of an hour before we are shown the protagonist, Sujata—and it is with a song idealising *bachpan* (childhood). The story thus far: a child from the Dalit community (the film uses the word *achoot*, meaning untouchable) is adopted by a Brahmin couple. The father initiates the adoption but the mother cannot quite reconcile herself to loving this lower-caste child as much as her biological daughter. This is further exacerbated when the man chosen as a groom for their daughter falls in love with Sujata. Sujata decides to sacrifice her love to assuage her mother. But the family tensions are only finally resolved in the last sequence when the mother needs blood and Sujata generously donates her blood. Blood serves both as a modern medical image but also didactically refers to the fact that caste is a false separation within the human matrix.

In *Sujata*, many of Nutan's strengths are consolidated—she is pre-eminently a listener and thus a reactor (it is often said that the best acting is reacting). While cinema typically prioritises speaking and the content of speech, in *Sujata* the camera highlights and frames a listening subject. Key pieces of information in the plot that reveal secrets of identity, that hurt feelings and break hearts are mostly overheard and twists in the tale depend on how listeners react to truths being revealed to them. The convention of representing conversations in realist cinema is to show listening as a reaction shot. Bimal Roy and Nutan push the edges of that convention. The listening subject here is not only listening but is an epitome of active eloquence.

Sujata is primarily about caste-consciousness in India and the pathos is best conveyed through the timing and rehearsal of fine, apposite pauses, of learning to navigate the very recesses of the movements of rejection (and similar negative affects) and of still being able to retain a musicality of action even within the pain. The listening in the film becomes an art of articulation in itself—it is a deep absorption of the harsh realities of discrimination but it is also a building of resilience that will await its moment of assertion. Nutan manages to give a sense of listening (to difficult matters) even when her face is turned away. Her work is greatly complemented by Bimal Roy's increasing mastery—simple but beautiful framing, the starkness of lighting and shadows, the editing that can capture in its patience the slowest, slightest tilt of Nutan's head. In one of the key scenes of the film, she quietly leans against a blank white wall—this is when she overhears her mother saying her lover had agreed to marry her sister. It is that infinitesimal capture (against the starkness of wall—a repeated image in their next film *Bandini*) that allegorises the moment's crushing of spirit. Roy gives Nutan ample scope for acting (*abhinaya*)—facial close-ups, slow pacing, the enunciation of dialogue that allows for clarity, emphasis, tone and crucially, that quality of hesitation that makes words and speech sound most piercing and authentic. Further, Roy works with slim plots—there is thus more scope for the unfolding of acting. As the editor for *Mahal* he had already allowed those extra seconds for the frame, was in no hurry to cut, and so his best work (reminiscent of the older generation auteurs like V. Shantaram) still carry the memory of the movies as a sequence of stills, of photographs, of a stillness that resides in the heart of movement.

It is worth noting that Nutan's first appearance in *Sujata* puts a clear onus on the camera to build a relationship with her character—it has to look for her, demonstrate affinity, build trust. The camera glides in from the gate of a single story colonial bungalow (named *Charu Vilaas* after the mother), past a sweeper clearing the path with a broom and another domestic help scurrying at the back; the viewer can grasp the vista of the path and as the camera enters the house, to the notes of a piano. The camera moves towards the piano, then there is a faux-reveal (it is of the sister), the male domestic help has come to the sister to ask for Sujata—he is told she is hanging clothes after doing the laundry. The camera now shifts to the roof where the help enters the frame calling Sujata's name and the camera pans to a sari hanging on a clothesline—the expanse of the sari serving as a screen-within-a-screen that projects a working woman's shadow. Her smiling face is revealed only after the sari is pulled down.

Much is established by this introduction—Sujata is attending to domestic labour (in alliance with the sweeper below and the domestic help) and in contrast to the blithe piano-playing sister, Rama. She is revealed first as a shadow—a reference both to being in the shadow of the family's love, as well as anticipating the awkward black-face make-up that the film inconsistently maintains for her (reaffirming the stereotype of the Dalit as dark-skinned). As Sujata converses with the help she is still performing the repetitive pleating of the sari and the conversation with the help is indeed on organising the household's morning routine. She is dressed too in a traditional mode (compared to the fashionably clad sister) but the camera lingers longer on Sujata. The sister below begins a song and the relay of the song through both women (the lyrics speak of a shared and happy childhood) uses fluttering fabric as visual transition. For one, it is fashionable clothing and curtains, for another it is labour—both solidarity and difference between the sisters is established. There is already a tense relationship of Sujata to the household—she is in the liminal space of the terrace (and later, she is mostly found in a greenhouse with plants). She is of the house and yet longs to break free, at least to the midway space of the garden. She can never quite possess the house in the sovereign manner of Rama at the piano. In the space of the terrace framed by trees during that first song as an adult, the viewer sees Sujata, chin to the sky, her gaze on a flight of birds, her neck upturned. There is already a coupling of the camera and face and later trajectories of the camera will find her in similar flowing sites: near rivers, under picturesque bridges, carefully watering the house-garden where *koel* (cuckoo) sounds seem to trail her. In moments of joyous singing, her face fills the frame as they intersperse with shots of nature (leaf, cloud, bird, flower) and both these types of images invite the viewer into a larger ambit of feeling.

The camera defines the distinct visual space of the sisters but it is essential to the plot that they are confused by strangers—one sister is often mistaken for the other. Even in the privacy of the house, Sujata walks with a bent head, in contrast to the carefree confidence of the sister. There are many occasions where Sujata has to react with hurt at being called '*beti-jaisi*' (like-a-daughter, instead of daughter) by her mother Charu. The camera makes a particular effort to accord her dignity and space, especially when the mother makes further comments such as her lack of education. After one of her mother's rude comments, Sujata is shown walking slowly up the stairs (the upper floor is her respite) with a shadow trailing beside her, a darkened, doubled self against a single plaintive line of music. A top-angle shot follows of Sujata sitting on her bed. She is lit from both sides maintaining the sharp black of the shadow, the bars of the bed and window falling strongly behind and on the bed suggesting imprisonment (Fig. 4). As she slowly raises her head the camera meets her at eye-level, glides to a close shot of her face, the background steadily darkening behind her. The next cut is to a painful childhood memory of her mother insisting that she is not her daughter but 'like a daughter'—a heartbreaking difference for a little girl that will carry to her adulthood as we see from the tears flowing down Sujata's face.

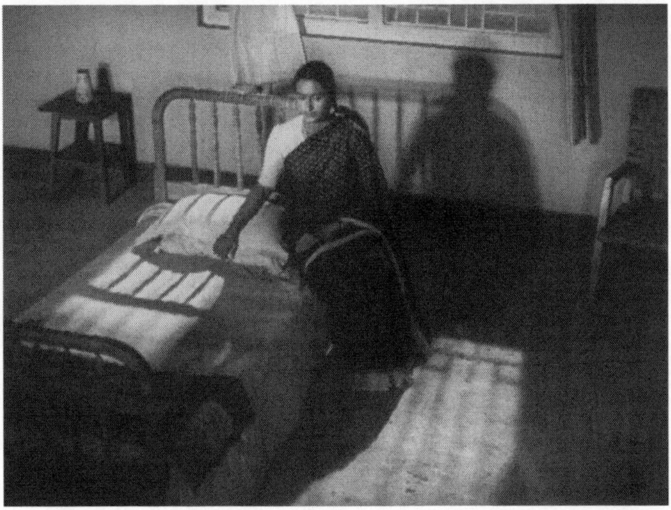

Fig. 4 *Source NFAI*

This almost-daughter motif is repeated in the film to show the strain between the adopted untouchable girl and the high-caste mother. It recurs with every introduction of Sujata to a new person who enters their domestic space. Sujata continues to occupy the position of the listener responding to her mother by sorrowful silence or exiting the scene. It is hence important that when first introduced to Adheer (the male love interest played by Sunil Dutt, who is the grandson of a conservative aunt), the reply to his simply query of who she is, results in her abruptly exiting the scene. She turns anxious, walks away alone in a long shot with her back to us, silhouetted, with another accompanying shadow emerging on the wall. The mother later says that the respectable stay away from even the 'shadow of the untouchable'. The walking away in response to imminent or casual unkindness of the inner or extended family is a characteristic visual trope. The depth of the moment owes both to the lighting, editing, as well as Nutan's expert reaction shots to any question of identity. It is a trauma she has to revisit every time a stranger comes on the scene and it locks her up further in the kitchen and tea-making labour, as opposed to the conversation and the living room. There is little she can do beyond turning away from the oppressiveness of caste within the extended family, of having to live amongst those who will, at some critical point, humiliate. When Sujata brings tea for Adheer and the aunt, the mother tells her to get the cook Madhav (of higher status than her) to re-make the tea. If in *Bandini*, she is in a real prison, here it is in the gilded prison of family.

After Adheer leaves, Sujata leans against the wall outside her parents' room, listening to the conversation about her untouchability. Her listening is now familiar to the viewer but the visual construction of the scene suggests that this is going to be a different kind of listening—a difficult truth will have to be encountered but only after Sujata speaks aloud for the first time the question that has always been trapped in her silence. The sequence strongly underlines this relationship between speech and listening. As her mother comes out of the room, Sujata asks: 'Who am I?' As the mother avoids the question, Sujata steps ahead into the light, coming into focus and foreground—the shadow occupies the space where she had stood (Fig. 5.1). It is as if she has stepped out of her own shadow—her posture is defiant. She repeats the difficult words with clarity: 'Who am I?' As her mother seeks to evade her question and walk away, Sujata follows her, insisting on an answer. The two women are now the only players in the taut domestic arena—there is a panel of crisscrossing black and white lines dividing them (Fig. 5.2).

Fig. 5.1 *Source NFAI*

Fig. 5.2 *Source NFAI*

In the over-the-shoulder shot that follows, the camera is behind the mother who will finally reveal the truth. Yet, though the strength of words belongs to the mother, the camera is more nurturing of the listening face that is lit softly against a neutral grey wall. 'You are an untouchable,' says the mother and this is followed by a close reaction-shot of Sujata's palms springing back from her mother's hands. The camera returns to its watch over the mother's shoulder as Sujata walks backwards, away from the lens, her shadow on the wall moving with her, forming a third figure between her and her mother. The truth about her biological parents (who are dead) is again revealed in a powerful visual configuration—the two women in profile facing each other but not in eye contact. As unkindness piles on unkindness, Sujata absorbs this in a close shot, a slow turn of her face from the listening profile to the speaking frontal view and repeats the word '*bojh*' (burden) as her gaze lowers in pain. The shot which started with her profile moving from the right of frame (through a continuous motion and bend of the head that emotes through throat and eyes) against a backdrop of a grilled window ends with her face sliding out from the left of frame. It is a long exit, her face sustaining the pain. Pointedly, the shot does not end with her exit. One continues to watch the window—it now shows rain and lightning on a dark night with fluttering shadows of vegetation, revealed as a plantain leaf bent by relentless rain. The painful listening that Sujata has endured is shared with the elements—an affinity of the character with nature is developed through the film through images of gardens and skies and river.

With the rain, the sequence shifts outdoors. Sujata's feet and silhouette are seen walking in rain and darkness towards the river and an under-bridge that had been established earlier in the film. This public space contains a large mural dedicated to the memory of Mahatma Gandhi against which Sujata leans. The rain is loud, she raises her head slowly, as though unbearably heavy, she clutches her chest, her long fingers alive—it is an extraordinary depiction of despair, her whole body kindled into movement akin to the scene in *Seema* where she emotes hunger and temptation with the play between her toes and the coin on the street. The viewer knows immediately that she is contemplating suicide and the camera plays with focusing and unfocusing its figures (waves, fluttering leaves, the shine of harsh artificial street-lighting) through a tightly edited montage. The camera moves towards her emotive use of fingers, creasing and uncreasing her sari. There are repeated intercuts which gather pace: fingers, eyes, streetlight, waves, lips, rain. Suicide seems imminent (by drowning in the river)—but then her sari gets caught in the lettering below the mural and she finds herself gazing at Gandhi's face, a message of endurance and dignity in sorrow. With her decision to return to life, the pacing of the sequence shifts—the rain seems slower, softer, her pupils and face move more slowly, the visuals and sound become more attuned to her psychic temper. She walks back home.

Except for a few scenes, such as the one described previously, the film is shot within the rooms and passageways of the house. The parents and sister have large parts of the house to themselves—the living room with the piano and outside, the worlds of sport and theatre that the sister Rama partakes of. The 'untouchable' cannot enter the outside world even as a member of the family group. A later scene has a birthday party with the entry of strangers into the house. It is clearer than ever that Sujata is an interloper in her own home. Though standing bejewelled and with flowers in her hair, (with her make-up extra dark) she is often re-traumatised because guests do think of her as a biological daughter and are then curtly reminded by the mother that she is not. Sujata stands silently, welcoming people—her sister is at the centre of a group of friends, animated and laughing. It is later revealed, through another cut to childhood, that her birthdays are not celebrated. While her sister sings at the piano and the friends claim the living room with their group dances, Sujata walks and sits in the dark outside, vulnerable to alienation—it is only in the small greenhouse outside, amid large-leaved plants and wooden framings that she is unencumbered. This is where Adheer and she become aware of their feelings for each other. Sujata can act the role of both being dutiful part of the house (cook and gardener and *dhobi*), as well as enact an apartness, a separateness, a weight and sorrow of distance from the house such that even the father's kindness or Adheer's reverential, romantic love, cannot really breach.

Sujata is yet again privy to a private conversation—she overhears her mother's desire for Rama to marry Adheer. After a brief moment of hope, Sujata is again crushed, her head falling back into her shadow on the wall, a silence and darkness descending on the house. She again ascends the stairs with a sense of the weight of her ill-starred fate. The phone rings: she is startled but picks it up. It is Adheer who wants to sing to her—what follows is a finely choreographed song (*Jalte hai jiske liye*). The telephone allows the unexpected and complete mismatch of affect—he is buoyant and hopeful for their future but she is in despair. The use of the telephone (a medium of pure sound with no accompanying visual cue) highlights the centrality of listening to the plot and further, the listening for the unspoken. The song depicts the wooing male protagonist in a conventional manner, in that the choreography edits by the line of the lyric and the singing face. But Sujata's listening and disconsolate face is captured in innovative ways. Some frames show her dwarfed at the bottom edge, others magnify her from a low angle. The camera continues to be attuned to every flicker of her lashes, the silence of every tear that drops and each suppressed sigh. There is a sense of entrapment—she inhabits the negative space of the song, the muted pain constructed by many close-ups (tears, fingers and lips biting the edge of the sari). Adheer is unaware of her suffering until she indicates at the end of the song that she does not wish to continue the courtship.

The high point of the film may not be the ending—the film ends with the mother accepting Sujata because Sujata gave her blood when the mother suffers a medical emergency. Much of the last half hour makes for strained viewing as the plot seeks to reaccommodate her within the traditional family format. What is of greater visual interest is an earlier scene between Adheer and Sujata. Following the courtship song on the phone and the abrupt rejection, Adheer comes to the garden to 'reach a final decision' ('*faisla karne aaya hoon*'). The framing is typical of the posture of defiance that Nutan takes—it is reminiscent of the scene in *Seema* when she faces the gates of the *ashram* with her back and arms providing a counterpoint to a watchful noncommittal camera. In *Sujata*, Bimal Roy projects Nutan against the leafless branch of a stark tree, a contrast with the leafy gardens shown in the past—and even though the male protagonist is standing literally on high ground, it is Nutan who draws the viewer's eye with her fierce stance.

Sujata tells Adheer that they can never be married because he comes from a higher caste—this, of course, is of no significance to Adheer. 'I am an untouchable'—she announces, looking off the frame—that is not at either the viewer or Adheer. There is thus an affirmation of her identity and self-possession in her stance, a grace, understanding and strength. She is convinced by his silence that he will never come near her or wish to marry her. Only the audience is privy to the gentle smile on Adheer's listening face, a reassurance that her caste is of no significance to him. He follows her to the greenhouse and tries to convince her of his indifference to caste. Roy makes masterful use of the latticework of the greenhouse to highlight the speaking and listening of two figures across a tragic gulf of social inequalities—she is closer to the lens, her hands clutching the lattice that divides her shadowed face and he is bracing himself for rejection. It is this divide that the film tries to argue can be overcome, whether through sacrifice or repentance, as is seen in the final resolution when the mother no longer says 'like a daughter' but embraces Sujata as her own. On hearing 'daughter', the word Sujata had sought all her life, her listening is finally consummated.

Captive Desires

Bimal Roy's 1963 film *Bandini* is his most celebrated with its clutch of awards, such as the National Film Award for best Hindi film, as well as Best Actress (for Nutan) and Best Director. It was Roy's seventh win as Director (a record still unbroken) and Nutan's fifth (a record that lasted many decades)—Meena Kumari (discussed in the last chapter) remained a close contender with four wins. *Bandini* has many memorable frames and the expertise of Roy (and cinematographer Kamal Bose who had also worked in *Sujata*) in retaining a primordial stillness within the movement of the 'movie' image reaches fruition. Though no frame is a photograph in an intrinsic sense, there is great art in the ability to evoke immobility in a moving image and thus reference the older, pre-filmic history of photography. A particular skill is required in the clarity of cut in motion that memorialises image as both movement and stillness—the credits for example run against a background of photos of prison life and labour (stills from the film). *Bandini* conjures that world of grey tones, architecture and sparseness.

The film is not just in black and white as a technological convention but uses black and white spaces with self-conscious austerity—there are large blanks of colour (especially of prison walls, vertical black prison bars, black lines on a white sari, white bars of the metal hospital bed) that speak of an avowed moral depth as if black and white have an intrinsic allegorical quality. Realism here is bareness, a simple, uncluttered lyricism that allows the unadorned geometry of black and white to piercingly claim the viewer's eye. Such an effect is not just a particular visual aesthetic but also key to the story of *Bandini* centred on Kalyani, a woman prisoner (*bandini* means one who is bound)—and prison, perhaps more than anything, is that pooling of time, the stasis that interrupts and undermines the flow of everyday morality and convention. In a sense, prison is a rare collectivity—for here, as represented most notably in clothing and hair, the agents are made to surrender all their previous identity so that they can look similar and be made to labour at similar tasks. Differences are believed to be eradicated and names are replaced by numbers. Given such a premise, part of the challenge of the film is to make Kalyani (which ironically means auspicious) stand out.

Both age and youth clarify Nutan—in the eight years from Gauri in *Seema* to Kalyani in *Bandini*, one can see the evolution of her acting, especially her *abhinaya* (facial expressiveness)—whereas in *Seema* she acted more with her body, in *Bandini* one can see her use both face and body with equal facility.

The black and white palette of the film is firmly restrained and reiterative—black imposed on black, white imposed on white. This forces the eye to stay with the effects of both the density of blackness and the bleached quality of whiteness. In the first scene inside the prison, the women convicts are shown huddled in dark clothes in their ill-lit confines, their mouths covered due to fear of infection (one of the prisoners is vomiting blood)—the women look fearful and are shown shouting and spitting. When asked if anyone would help the ill woman, they collectively put their head down and keep silent. Though the gathering has several able women, they seem too afraid or cautious to volunteer to look after the ill. This is when a distinct voice rises from the crowd—'I am ready'. The blanketed faces part to reveal a mid shot of Kalyani's face, eyes averted and face calm, in contrast to the reaction of fellow-prisoners in the same frame. The impressed prison doctor Devendra (played by the actor Dharmendra) cautions her about the risks of caring for someone with an infectious disease. Kalyani steps forward and the crowd of women part, her eyes remain downcast as she speaks—her voice is firm and clear in thought and resoluteness. She then turns, exits the frame and returns with a document whereby they may assign her the caretaking service. The women cluster again, bonded in their scepticism of her boldness—they are also aligned with the woman jailer in their harshness of speech. Kalyani is thus established in contrast to everyone—there is her on one side and the collectivity (that includes the prison staff) on the other. This latter side is full of the minute hierarchies of jail life, of aggression, envy and thoughtlessness. The dark backdrop of the night, the dark blankets, the dark coats of the jailer and doctor only highlight the luminous calm resolve on Kalyani's face.

As if to reiterate this aforementioned stylistic decision of emphasising black-on-black and white-on-white aesthetics, the next scene is predominantly white and bleached. Bright sunlight bounces off the white uniforms of two men carrying a white cot, as Kalyani walks into the frame, white sari with black strikes, a long single plait of hair, facing away from the viewer.

In service, she seems resourceful, strong and is not overtly coy in the growing affinity that Devendra professes for her and indeed openly acknowledges his kindness. Though the plot has not yet revealed her past, one senses a return to a life before incarceration, a life of determination and clarity. Kalyani seems unembarrassed, even unconscious of being in jail. A direct gaze would signify mutuality in love but this would be unrealistic given the difference in status, the time-period of the film, etc. However, she does not move away when the doctor moves closer to her. Her neck bends gracefully, the eyes are downcast—but she talks easily, assertively, aware of the dignity that even the prisoner must demand, often going up to Devendra herself. This is just as her body stiffens (even as face and breathing register humiliation) against another jail authority's unwarranted flirtation. Prison clothes preclude the *ghoonghat* (traditional veiling). This first intimacy with Devendra over illness is mirrored in the last scene where Kalyani again chooses to nurse an ill lover instead of marrying the youthful Devendra.

Kalyani's profile is given prominence in the film—from behind her shoulder and in low angle in the plane closest to the camera, by the bars of the hospital window, waiting for the doctor, confiding in her friend and so on. The profile allows her to not have to always look down (the prisoner's shame or a woman's coyness). The 'halfness' of the profile speaks of a desire for invisibility or minimum visibility, an indirectness, even from Devendra. This indirectness also represents the enigma that Kalyani remains to the viewer—her crime is not revealed until late into the film. The play of visibility is clearest in the scene where Devendra declares his love: When he talks to her she slips behind the door. She is now only voice—facing the viewer, though her gaze and address are beyond. She has to reject his love though it is not without a sense of melancholy. The line of his arm can still be seen—an arm that represents that respectability, assurance and love that part of her must crave (Fig. 6.1). And on the other side of the ajar door, she is hidden to us, except for the fingers that clutch the door (Fig. 6.2). Roy constantly uses this idea of a door or partition with Kalyani on one side. It is a plot-point (it is used to overhear or create coincidences, etc.) but, more importantly, it helps concretise her split relation to the world and the figures that inhabit that respectable world. Her profile and the use of natural splits in the screen such that she cannot directly see what is in the other room is also extensively used in the last sequence of the film. In a series of painterly frames she is depicted as waiting for the steamer: she is listening and watching patiently, allowing her fate to, as it were, work itself in and through her.

Fig. 6.1 *Source NFAI*

Fig. 6.2 Source NFAI

The rhythm of labour and the enclosed spaces of the prison creates unexpected solitudes as well as alliances and friendships in prison, both between prisoners as well as between prisoners and jailers. The large blank walls and small bolted cells create an affect of large interior spaces within and between people—the space of the prison seems timeless, the homogeneity of clothing makes everything utopian (utopia in the original meaning of no-space). A sense of the hour and the locus (where is this prison?) slip away and though there are quarrels between inmates, it is also an enabler of whispered conversation, secrets, affirmations and insights. The life of a prisoner is more than the number of years of their sentence or the event of their crime—the interior space of the prison churns a deeper, more uninhibited melancholy, a greater openness to nature. Birds or flowers or the bars of a window or hospital bed turn instantly symbolic in the space and light of the prison. There is a sense of expansive time, even a melancholy sensuousness of time being eked out by the minute. Indeed, Nutan's best work is as this actor of profound homelessness, of being quite unable to even access a happy memory of home—it is only in the spaces of the prison or *ashram* (or the plant-filled greenhouse in *Sujata*) that she can imagine friendship or romance.

After being turned down by Kalyani, Devendra leaves the jail and soon after comes one of the most poignant song visualisations of Hindi cinema. The slow melodious song in a female voice (with barely any percussion) is composed (both lyric and music) in the idiom of a traditional *bidai* song, the song that laments the separation of a girl from her natal home, her longing to be reunited with her parents—*Ab ke baras bhej bhaiya ko babul* (This year, my father sends my brother to fetch me). The flat, tall whitewashed prison walls come to stand for the prison of marriage and the world outside with its promise of romance becomes the parental hearth. The image of a miniaturised solitary woman in white sitting in a pool of sunlight, her bent back to us, against the pale towering walls of the prison sets the mood of the song (Fig. 7.1). She turns sharply as a singing voice is heard. The singer is a forlorn fellow-prisoner, engrossed in the repetitive labour of the *chakki* (the stone that grinds grain). The patch of sunlight expands, the white palette spreads to include the floor and the singer—there is no room for a sky in this captive space (Fig. 7.2). The viewer/listener is dissolved into the song organically—the frame and rhythm step into the images and beat of the labour of the *chakki*. It is a slow song, dripping eternity into the lyric motion of a generous, flowing hand. As Charlie Chaplin, one of the virtuosos of black and white cinema who defiantly resisted the aesthetics of colour and sound as long as he could, reminds us in his autobiography: 'Placement of camera is cinematic inflection'.[10] He goes on to challenge the expectation that close-up gives more emphasis than a long shot and claims 'a close-up is a question of feeling; in some instances, a long shot can effect greater emphasis'.[11] It is an observation that is supported by the placement of camera and choice of lens in Bimal Roy's films, especially in the song being discussed. Long shots are less of distance but rather evoke intimacy and intensity of emotion, even as close shots may sometimes encourage dissociation and detachment in the viewer.

Fig. 7.1 Source NFAI

Fig. 7.2 Source NFAI

This song, more than anywhere else in the film, is treated as a series of stills, where the weight of labour is captured by unusual camera-angles (mostly low-angles) and where Kalyani's sensitive reserve is equally captured by her proximity to walls and fellow-prisoners caught in the portraitures of sorrow and memory. These are the images used when the credits had rolled at the beginning of the film—they include particularly fine images of older women: waiting, lonely, sorrowful women against walls, windows and iron bars. The relentlessly moving *chakki* is the only motion that spills from frame to frame. When the sky does make an appearance in the song, Kalyani's head is turned to it and the line of her neck speaks of her ache (Fig. 8). The viewer wonders: What is Kalyani's crime, how did she end up here?

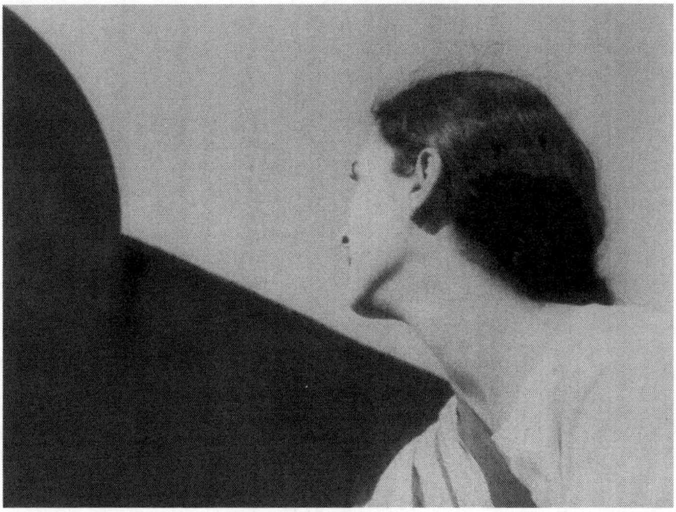

Fig. 8 *Source NFAI*

The scene after the song has her in the chief jailer's office where she requests that she not be freed as she has nowhere to go. The jailer is puzzled and asked why she inexplicably spurned the good doctor—he wants to know the whole story. What follows is an extraordinary long take of over a minute and a half. It begins with a steady mid-long shot with the jailer in the foreground to the right of the viewer as Kalyani starts to narrate the story of her family. The camera tracks forward and past the jailer to a mid shot of Kalyani, just as she recounts the particular fateful event of her beloved brother's death. Neither the shot nor the narrative of tragedy breaks and the camera continues to stay on her as she sits down on the floor with sorrow, covering her mouth with her hands. Throughout that moment of storytelling, slowly gathering sorrow in its remembrance, Kalyani seems to discover the words as she speaks them in their full tremulousness. Her face and body respond to the language unfolded by her lips, even as she is aware of the presence of another. As an actor Nutan has to synchronise the telling with the awareness of the movement of the camera as it inches towards her. The whole story told in a single shot up till the final collapse in tears, is a carefully graded performance—to control the loss of control is the key to fine acting. Nutan modulates her performance, pacing her plain speech and tone without self-pity, yet expressing emotion.

In some ways, the backstory and plot have only now begun: it is about one-third into the film already. This delay in contextualisation is what gives the film the sense of a slow unfolding, a sense of an internal and isolated crystal world of a woman prisoner's enigmatic subjecthood. Even away from prison bars, when depicting her past, the border between her subjectivity and any other person's is often imaged by barriers—for example, barbed wire. It is through barbed wire that she first looks at the house where the political revolutionary Bikash Ghosh (played by veteran actor Ashok Kumar) had been interred. The frames foreground at some length the wire against her body and face—especially the face as it glides within the blank white spaces between the wires, a relation of face and wire, sweetness and authority. This scene illustrates Nutan's mastery of knowing how to position herself vis-a-vis the camera—the zigzagging barbed wire necessitates a finesse of movement, an awareness of an irregularly and sharply sliced screen space (Fig. 9). The engagement of the actor with the camera is thus rendered more dynamic and active—she is gazing back, preserving interiorities and privacies that the camera cannot easily invade or capture.

Fig. 9 *Source NFAI*

In her house, she can often glimpse Ghosh only through the mesh in the door when he and her father are talking. Later, the barbed wire returns in the song as she keeps visiting his compound in the hope of seeing him. There are also bars in the small, floor-level window in her kitchen from where she observes the world or talks to friends. Bars at the window are prominently framed the night she nurses Ghosh when he is ill (this, of course, causes a fateful scandal that eventually makes her leave the village). There are further shadows of bars on the walls that night and many other interior spaces of houses she inhabits invoke these strips of verticality within the frame. Lastly, there are the bars through which the welding takes place—this is the site where she commits the fateful murder.

The murder is the fulcrum of the film's narrative because it has to elicit compassion from the viewer rather than moral judgement. Circumstances have landed the destitute Kalyani at a hospital where she has to do menial labour including tending to abusive patients. Kalyani patiently bears all the tantrums and cruelty but is gradually pushed to the limits of her endurance. On the day of the murder, she loses her father to a road accident—when she is shown her father's corpse, it is a long shot again. Her face is unmoving. Grief will register less on her face than the rageful actions that follow and this delayed reaction of dazed events (culminating in the murder) adds depth and dimension to the film. The sequence is shot in a manner that should by now be familiar—there is the slow ascent of a staircase (as in *Sujata*), strong shapes of shadow and strips of light, harsh voices and commands that pile up the injustice on an already vulnerable psyche. It is this event of murder (but also this event as a terminus to her life of deeply undeserved injustice and sorrow) that defines the enigma of the character of the woman prisoner that the film opened with. One can understand why such a woman cannot marry a simple-souled doctor.

To retrace the steps on the day of the murder: after the shock and numbness of losing her father, she returns to her work to face a particularly temperamental and bitter woman patient who had been long abusing her. But on this day, she makes a second shocking discovery—the woman is married to Ghosh, the man she had loved and who had inexplicably left her. Kalyani is pushed and humiliated by the woman, the tray and cup in her hand are kicked and smashed to the floor. Roy orchestrates a seamless transition from these traumatic external events to the state of the character's mind: as the camera inches closer to Kalyani's pain-filled face and narrowing eyes, a sustained shrill sound takes over—it might be a train whistle but the following shot suggests a welding machine (Fig. 10.1). The shadows of window bars behind her add to the psychological tautness and desperation of the moment. There are labourers at work on metal beyond her window and the sparks and clamour set the mood for the distress that will manifest and exhaust itself in crime (Fig. 10.2). Roy and Nutan work effectively with the window bars and crisscrossed lights on the face as signalling that moment of breakdown and collapse (Fig 10.3). Even before entering prison, it seems that much of the framing (of her face, viewpoint or body) have been composed by bars or barbed wire, so there is a final culminating appositeness and even ineluctability in her ending up in prison. As Kalyani watches the sparks of the welder, the silhouetted back of her head fills the frame and lights flicker (Fig. 10.4). She turns around menacingly. The moment returns to a realistic space with the ensuing long shot, even as her posture remains the same. This is also true of the welding at the back.

Fig. 10.1 *Source NFAI*

Fig. 10.2 *Source NFAI*

Fig. 10.3 *Source NFAI*

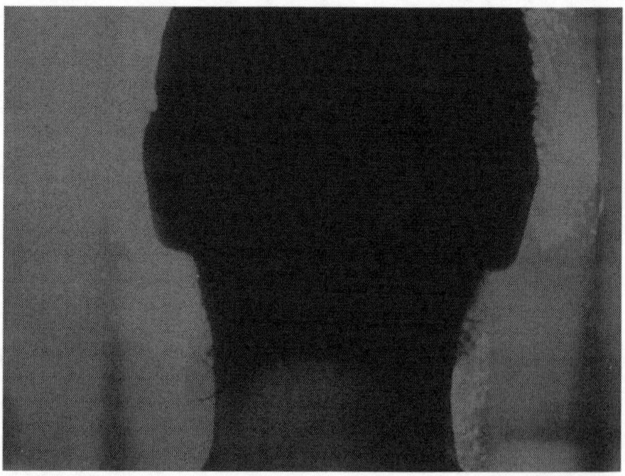

Fig. 10.4 *Source NFAI*

As the abusive patient shouts her name, the viewer knows that Kalyani's psyche is unraveling: she stands in the distance framed through the banisters of wooden stairs. A return to the previous close shot of her in profile against the glare of the welding takes us back to her state of mind. The shriek of the metalwork clamours again. The camera watches warily from a low angle, then zooms in as Kalyani bends over the flame of the stove to make tea for the patient. The frame dissolves to Kalyani walking away from the window with the cup of tea, her eyes to the right of frame and the point of view is a close shot of a bottle labelled 'poison'. In a frame that includes the numbed Kalyani in profile and her reflection in the glass of the cupboard, lights continue to flicker. Close shots of two objects overlap in the next frame—the white cup and the black bottle of poison. This is when the shrill sound dies out to clicks and what sounds like a sigh. The visual is of a frame that alternates between pitch black and the fiery light of the welders at work—the few seconds of silence in the sequence seem more piercing than the pounding of machines. The tempo of the sound picks up again as Kalyani's sari moves past the bottle of poison, the light continuing to flash on the bottle. Kalyani walks down the stair in robotic motion, strong lines (of stairs, ceiling, door and shadow) ominously filling up the frame. As soon as Kalyani exits the frame the metallic sounds stop, the frame dissolves slowly to the fluttering curtains of the patient's door, the lighting indicating that there has been a time-lapse. Silence is all that is left of the crime. The triumph of the scene is as much in the precision of the psychologised images (such as the agitation of the welding), as in the pacing and juxtaposition of individual shots.

Having disclosed the compounded stresses that led to the murder, the film is left with the moral question of whether the prisoner deserves a fresh start in life—should she be rehabilitated into sanctioned domesticity? The plot quickly arranges for this to happen—the doctor and his mother invite her home, displaying magnanimity and indicating prospective marriage. However, on her way to that promised domesticity, Kalyani faces one last temptation. As she waits for the train, she runs into an ailing man in the waiting room who is revealed to be Ghosh. It is also revealed that he had only left her for what he believed was a larger, public good—in truth, he had remained devoted to her in his heart. Kalyani is torn and in one final frame in a bare waiting room of screens and wooden partition, the two sit silently, the rest of their life rendered wholly uncertain (Fig. 13). It as if they are each ensconced in their private, contrived solitudes—each in their own prison-niche, trapped in separable fates.

Fig. 11 Source NFAI

Though Kalyani does eventually choose Ghosh, it is the frames pertaining to their paired solitudes that the camera lingers over, amplifying and prolonging them, providing the affect of separation (*viraha*) that is so central to the aesthetic of the film. For Roy, even in films not discussed in this chapter, such as *Devdas* and *Madhumati*, what is emotive is less the formulaic conventions of the happy union at the end and more the visual elongation of separation, imprisonment, the impossibilities of yearning and distance. This chapter has argued for a minimalist Roy aesthetics that poignantly highlighted visual affects of separation and impossibilities made possible by Nutan's responses to his framing. However, there is another model for that visual affect in the same historical moment of the late 1950s. That model belongs to Guru Dutt—and this is even though at first glance, Roy and Dutt could not be more different. Whereas Roy helmed an aesthetic of minimalism and astute pacing, Guru Dutt accomplishes similar meditations on loss and longing—but in an aesthetic of sharp contrasts of light and dark (studiously avoiding Roy's favoured spectrum of grays). Further, as will be seen, the editing in Guru Dutt's films highlights an artist's passionate movement. This may be contrasted to Roy's slow precision which aspired to the stillness of the photograph in order to actualise the inner, un-transcendable destitutions of a woman prisoner or unloved child.

Framing the Artist: Guru Dutt's *Pyaasa* (1957) and *Kaagaz ke Phool* (1959)

Nearly a decade after Raj Kapoor applied cinematic language to the theme of unbridled ambition (and inevitable isolation) of the artistic temperament in his first film *Aag*, the same dynamic (of thematic and visual language) accomplishes its full flowering with Guru Dutt's *Pyaasa* (The Thirsty, 1957). Since its release and box office success, this film has basked in the adulation of generations of audiences as well as the critical attention of scholars.[1] Several images from *Pyaasa* (images that are suspended in latticed shadows) have become metonymic for the black and white visuality of Hindi cinema. Film historians have commented on the socialist underpinnings of the trope of the 'thirsty' artist (starved for food as well as respect) in an uncaring, punishing world and have acknowledged the sharply delineated light and shade of V.K. Murthy's cinematography as a key contribution to Guru Dutt's oeuvre.[2] For Guru Dutt, as for his viewers, there is one elusive question that becomes the heart of *Pyaasa*: If the nature of art is to challenge and decentre social orthodoxy and prejudice even as it is acutely marginalised, how does one begin to claim that blighted centre? In the claiming of the centre is the sharper quandary—how does one visually frame the artist? This predicament of the framing—the outcaste opposed to the establishment, the artistic opposed to the materialist—becomes resolved within the celluloid rectangle. The most emblematic image of this film—the artist silhouetted against an over-lit doorway, both arms stretched like a man on a crucifix or a bird readying for flight, gazing down at the dark multitudes—becomes that resolution: the liminal figure paradoxically placed at a new centre, the last rows of the theatre as opposed to the centre of the stage.

The initial plotline for *Pyaasa* involved a painter, not a poet, to be essayed by Dilip Kumar. Guru Dutt decided to play the lead role after Dilip Kumar failed to turn up on the first day of the shoot, not wanting to play a character apparently similar to the protagonist of Dilip Kumar's earlier film *Devdas.*[3] As painting gets replaced by poetry, one is invited to consider the introspective cadence of film-making. The entire body of verse in the film (whether set to music or not) came from the pen of a single poet who becomes the invisible alter ego of Vijay, the protagonist of *Pyaasa*—this was Sahir Ludhianvi (1921–1980). An anti-establishment poet who brought both his socialist sensibilities and his Urdu-infused intricate compositions into the realm of popular cinema[4], Ludhianvi was widely known by his *nom de plume*, Sahir (meaning magician). Just as Sahir Ludhianvi reputation as a temperamental genius added to the mystique of the film, so did the mythography of Guru Dutt's career in the Bombay film industry—an eerie blurring of life and art. Coming from a middle-class family that gave Guru Dutt no entitlements in the film industry and beginning his career as a dancer with Uday Shankar's India Cultural Centre, his public persona emerged through a series of film projects through the 1940s (as an actor or as crew) leading to his first directorial debut in 1951 with *Baazi* (Gamble). Abrar Alvi, Guru Dutt's close professional associate for over a decade, calls him 'a man obsessed with cinema'[5] who insisted on complete involvement in the visual design and execution of every shot in the films he directed.[6] Through the 1950s, Guru Dutt directed a series of films, many of them commercial successes,[7] till the box-office failure of *Kaagaz ke Phool* (Paper Flowers, 1959)—the last film to carry his name as director. As his biographer Nasreen Munni Kabir records, public narratives of his life continued to be rife with rumours of a temperamental disposition and an extra-marital romantic obsession—this only fuelled the image of the misunderstood artist.[8] There were reported suicide attempts. Guru Dutt continued to act and produce films till his sudden death in 1964 from a drug overdose that may or may not have been deliberate.

Through his screenplays as well as his life choices, Guru Dutt remains the quintessential mercurial artist whose framing, even when it dethrones the norm of the 'hero', is in truth also an affirmative embrace of finitude and human limit. Screen narratives seem to presciently turn into life narratives and there is a multiplication of different kinds of death on and off screen—social annihilation (*Pyaasa*), destitute death (*Kaagaz ke Phool*), professional demise (Dutt refusing to direct after the failure of one film) and Dutt's own eventual suicide/death at the age of thirty-nine. This chapter makes a case to read *Pyaasa* and *Kaagaz ke Phool* as meta-cinema, not just in the biographical sense or as cinema-about-cinema or art-about-art (all these are anyways explicitly thematised) but to read the visual language (in partnership with his cinematographer V.K. Murthy) as the extraordinarily self-conscious carving out of an affective visual language of solitude that haunts the very interiority of the frame.

One might begin with a brief explication of the plot of the two films: *Pyaasa* is the story of a talented, struggling poet Vijay (played by Guru Dutt) who is unable to get support from his family or the publishing industry and spends most of his time on the streets. A sensitive sex-worker Gulab (played by Waheeda Rehman) falls in love with Vijay and his verse. In parallel, Vijay runs into his college sweetheart Meena (Mala Sinha) who is now married to a wealthy publisher Mr Ghosh (Rehman). The successful publisher does not miss any opportunity to humiliate Vijay. Disgruntled with his life, Vijay decides to commit suicide. But, by chance, a beggar who tries to save him is killed—earlier Vijay had given the beggar his coat. With Vijay assumed to be dead (he is soon to be put away in a mental asylum for claiming to be himself), the scene is set for the publisher and relatives of the poet to make Vijay a 'posthumous' literary hero for their own financial benefit. Vijay escapes from the asylum only to witness the hypocrisy and selfishness of the world. He chooses to abandon fame as well as the corrupt orders of family, society and even art. *Kaagaz ke Phool* has a similar plotline of the rise and fall of the artist's fortunes but this time the protagonist is a film director Suresh Sinha (again played by Guru Dutt) who is looking for a new face to play the role of Paro in his rendition of the beloved Bengali novel *Devdas*. While Suresh is professionally successful, his personal life is difficult—he is estranged from his wife and is in litigation for custody rights to his young daughter who is in boarding school. Suresh finds a kindred spirit in Shanti (Waheeda Rehman), who is cast in the role of Paro and the film goes on to become a hit. However, due to his daughter's jealous interference, Shanti has to emotionally step away from Suresh who descends into alcoholism and penury after losing the custody battle. Even though Shanti returns to the film industry to help Suresh, he refuses and ultimately dies anonymously on the same studio floor where he once created cinematic masterpieces.

It can be argued that these two films, *Pyaasa* and *Kaagaz ke Phool*, not only follow each other (1957 and 1959) but serve as inversions of each other. The exploited discarded poet of *Pyaasa* who finds belated fame is reversed as the successful film director who ends up unrecognised and penurious in *Kaagaz ke Phool*. The arrows of failure and success move in opposite directions but add up to the same result—an indictment of the heartlessness and myopia of both society and the artistic establishment. A case can also be made for reading the two films as continuous in their visual styling, a continuity of tonality achieved through lighting and camera movement. The language of the frame (in these two films) speaks for the artist's muted and thwarted aspiration—in other words, a distinct aesthetic of framing has been self-consciously carved out.

Deleuze in *Cinema 1* invites us to think of framing in different ways, of which the first two are especially germane to this book. The first is the classical notion of the frame as 'a relatively closed system which includes everything which is present in the image—sets, characters and props'.[9] The second is the idea of the frame as dynamic, as being carved even as the action unfolds to the eye—this is the frame as a 'dynamic construction in act', that which 'opens and shows the surroundings ... and functions as "visual accordion"'.[10] These dual meanings of framing—one, the image as contained in the rectangle of the cinematic frame and two, the synergy of dynamic constructions, openings and revelations—can be productively read in the two films discussed in this chapter. One would like to extend Deleuze's reading of the dynamic interior of the individual frame into the synergistic manner in which frame is conjoined to frame as both transition as well as a continuous affective threshold. Indeed, in this chapter, the readings specifically seek to achieve this through the following axes—(a) a central 'metaphoric' image (set, prop, figure or face) that anchors and resonates through the framing of the scene, (b) the visual unity and affective force in the pacing created by the movement from frame to frame within a large sequence (scene, song) and (c) a black and white palette that avoids diffused greys in favour of stark contrasts that celebrate the bleached white and the dense black, both clearly demarcated and formulated to give depth and volume.

The Anchor of Metaphor

In *Pyaasa*, the fiery and singed passion of the perpetually high-strung theatre artist in *Aag* (as discussed in the first chapter) turns into a gentle aqueous world of the not-worldly private poet, and this is strongly signalled in the opening sequence. The credit titles seem to float on water (white font on dark waters with white lotuses) and the first shot, post credits, is also of water. The title *Pyaasa* references thirst and the lack of water, an absence of validation for the contemporary poet. The credits end with a gentle pan and tilt up from water to shore. A disembodied male voice starts to recite a composition in the measured singsong delivery associated with Urdu poetry—*Ye hanste hue phool, ye mehka hua gulshan* (These smiling flowers, this fragrant garden). The scene attempts to orient its visual language (water, flowers, light and posture) to a poetic, textual sensibility. The romantic evocation (in the lyrics) of the bounties of nature ends with the wonderment of what the poet can possibly offer to such self-sustaining nature. All he has, the poet claims, are a few tears and a few sighs. Against this recitation, the frame fills with corresponding images—he sings of a bee and a bee is shown. The poet is not just one who mouths or prints lines but he is also visualised, embedded in the world—the film is this search for a cinematic language of poetic action. The camera tries to align with the lounging poet's point of view, though the camera also embraces a few other points—there are three quick cuts of flowers—and the point of view may then be seen as symbolic of a sensibility of continuity between nature and the poet, a continuity both in its creative invocations, as well as in its fragility (the lake and flowers are trapped in an urban-scape, the thirsty interloper bee gets crushed by an indifferent human foot). The poem/song may be composed in real time, or in memory—it is an unadorned singing, highlighting the words rather than composition or instruments. This will remain an important aspect of the film. Either way, the visuals are lined up to strengthen this initial establishment of his persona, the image thus integral to the lyric and the poetic self, the words not always lip-synched but drawn from a pervasive memory. The film establishes the negotiation of the nuts and bolts of both poetry and the visual from an overall affect—a perspective of a newly awakening wondrous world, a morn of possibility and hopefulness. This film, which prioritises mood, conveys effectively an opening idyll—the poet, vulnerable, hopeful, pleasantly drowsy, divorced from the urban world that awaits him. Therefore, the body and face of the watching, brooding, supine poet becomes the anchoring metaphor that strengthens an initial establishment of his persona (Fig. 1). It is his first and last patch of quiet, for he will soon have to get up and encounter the indifference and cruelty of the city and family.

Fig. 1 *Source NFAI*

From mulling in the lap of Edenic nature to jostling in the apathetic city, the poet has only hardship for company—an unsympathetic hearth and cruel siblings, humiliating rejections at publishing houses, homelessness and sleeping on open benches of public parks. This casting out of the poet is not only a signification of the marginalised stature of the artist in socio-economic spheres but is a mapping of the domain of youth (young men in a young nation) with all the limitations and aspirations inherent in that position. Abrar Alvi points out that most of the film crew of *Pyaasa* was under thirty years of age, including the director Guru Dutt who was about twenty-eight years old.[11]

The first sense of 'arrival' and respite for the viewer and the poet is when the poet finally reaches the space where he rightfully belongs—the public stage and the microphone. This narrative moment is approximately forty minutes into the storyline and the setting is a college reunion where the poet arrives with some misgivings. His clothes, for one, speak of his poverty. The long parallel tracking of the silhouetted poet as he walks along the dark corridor outside a well-lit hall builds anticipation towards a visual anchor for the scene. The central object (a metaphor of foiled artistic aspiration) is a large grooved steel microphone, prominently foregrounded and glinting in a top light—its presence is revealed as Vijay is announced. Persuaded to come on stage (depicted in flat lighting thus far), the poet stands beside the microphone that is framed between his face and a shimmer of light (that is new to the stage) across the left edge of the frame (Fig. 2.1). The camera swings towards the poet's eyes as they narrow with painful recognition. The next frame is his point of view and it is from a sympathetic lens that does not look down at the gathering from the elevation of the stage but instead offers a straight frontal view of a seated woman whose face is hidden by a sheet of paper. In a duplication of the previous closing in on the poet's eyes, the camera again swings in as the paper lowers and the woman's face is revealed to be that of the poet's old love (Fig. 2.2).

Fig. 2.1 *Source NFAI*

Fig. 2.2 *Source NFAI*

The poet's disturbed face fills up the screen, as does the microphone, now looming blurred in the foreground. Swift intercuts between their expressions establish the ache of old romance, the microphone the only confidante to this recognition. In fact, the microphone serves as the only interceding public—the people sitting in the chairs are excluded from the meeting of two solitary personae and memories. In *Pyaasa*, women are shown as triggers or readers of poetry and in contexts of recitation but never quite included in the creation of the art. Vijay's face and the microphone wobble as a friend pulls at his coat, urging him to recite something ('Vijay, *kuch sunao na*'). The recitation begins but the intimate moment of pain and longing is no longer private and it has become a more demanding performative moment—the angle of the camera and the lighting change as if in acquiescence, the microphone still negotiating this transition as the poet bends his face into his hand and begins to painfully draw out his words (Fig. 3).

Fig. 3 *Source NFAI*

The poetry speaks of being disillusioned by the struggles of life and the camera slowly moves back as he settles into the lines. The camera eye that had tracked back from the stage starts to move ahead into the audience in the next frame keeping the same pace. Now we have a second knowing (suspicious) eye—one row behind the woman loved by the poet is her husband who has spotted her consternation.

An audience member interrupts and taunts the poet for singing a depressing song. The poet responds by clutching the stand of the microphone—the object becomes more anthropomorphised, a supporter and a proxy lover. His grip never eases from the microphone as the song picks up in intensity. The relationship between the poet, his poetry and the stage (represented by the microphone in close shots) is that of conflict and exile. He is always alone in the frame, the harsh light casting shadows, for it is not enough that he is starving—he has to be actively humiliated. The camera continues to swing towards and away from him, always keeping the microphone in the frame—the partnership breaks only when the poet abruptly abandons the song and walks off the stage.

The first cinemascope film to be made in India, *Kaagaz ke Phool* continues with *Pyaasa*'s theme of the humiliated artist, but this time very consciously as meta-cinema—the artist is a film director and the studio forms an important narrative and spatial orientation for the visual aesthetics. V.K. Murthy talks about that first encounter with the wide-format which was at that time accomplished with a different anamorphic lens that was mounted as an attachment on the camera lens. Hence, it was an improvised lens while the negative stayed 35 mm.[12] The additional stretch in the horizontality of the frame is employed in this film from the very beginning with regard to its most central metaphor—the studio. The self-referentiality is in the very first shot of the film, a soaring bird's eye view (the camera moving up on a crane), a hovering panoptic eye that is all-seeing. It only pauses at the name board of the studio. This is a faux-credit in some ways for the production here is not of 'Ajanta Pictures' (as written on the gate) but of 'Guru Dutt Films', the 'real' credits that start to appear in the second shot of the film. This top angle frame 'looks down' at the ageing director through the feet of an oversized idol, one that indicates the grandiosity of traditional cinematic plotlines in India (mythology, for instance) and the flashy scale of entertainment culture (Fig. 3). It is also worth noticing the visual representation of the production space as a studio lot in the mode of Hollywood which was not quite the case in India at that time, an effort perhaps to evoke a studio culture. The strings in the background music add to the evocative mood of this initial setting. The credits on the screen reveal the crew to be mostly continuous with *Pyaasa* except for the noticeable replacement of Sahir Ludhianvi with another poet—Kaifi Azmi. The frame that follows the end of the credits is an indoor mirroring of the previous top-angle outdoor shot. This time the camera is inside the studio floor and on the catwalk, watching the director through the ramp and grid of wires, as he walks in through the over-lit doors that have become a hallmark of Murthy's visualisation (Fig. 4). The director's shadow is long and ominous.

Fig. 4 *Source NFAI*

As if to preempt the coldness and distance towards the director that might be caused by three sustained top-angle shots, the next frame is a low angle—the camera looking up from behind the director who in turn is looking at the ceiling of the studio, all metallic and geometric (Fig. 5). However, even when the figure is given stature (low angle) it has (a) made him frail and old and (b) it can easily swing back to technological gigantism. The film seems to need this relation of the protagonist to the art-form as dwarfing in a way that the poetry of

Pyaasa cannot achieve. Print is demure compared to the technological coldness and power of giant studio machinery. As metafiction, the camera cannot sink into the theatricality of action (of the artist-theme) but rather, into the theatricality of the medium (cinema). A cut-away image of a skylight adds to the ghostly timeless ambience (Fig. 5) even as the narrative voice-over is telling us that nothing changes in the atmosphere of the studio—only films and film-makers change. The director turns to walk out of the frame. Every shot in this opening sequence is oriented towards height—ladders, vertical intricate shadows on walls, the camera-eye looking up or down, the human figure moving/looking up or down—and this is in many ways a conscious anti-proscenium vantage, for the proscenium viewing is archetypally fixed and frontal.

Fig. 5 *Source NFAI*

In one of the most beautiful uses of chiaroscuro in sculpting space, the next frame is a wide shot of the director moving across the empty studio floor towards the steps leading to the lighting ramp above. As the director slowly walks up the stairs, cane in hand, the camera follows, keeping him company at an even pace. In an astonishing moment of surrender and poignancy, the camera watches the director from behind as he peers over the ramp and briefly we have an image of a headless man—a moment of abject solitude before he slowly raises his head. This fragile privacy is ruptured by a light that falls on him, soon followed by several other lights on the grid ahead. The studio has come to life. And with this begins the famous song of despair—*Dekhi zamaane ki yaari, bichade sabhi baari baari* (I have seen the friendship of the world, all scattered one by one). This initiates the first 'reveal' of the protagonist's face—bedraggled, unshaven and unkempt. The camera starts to move away from him simultaneously lowering (it is on a crane) and as it recedes the director is seen standing alone amidst a clutter of equipment and metal grids that hold lights—the bars of the ramp forming a sharp V at his stomach, as if impaling him in his isolation (Fig. 6).

Fig. 6 *Source NFAI*

In contrast to the chaotic grid of lights with its many wires, ramps and beams is the fluidity of the gliding camera made more fluid by the lilting non-percussive music composed of strings. As the plaintive song continues, the director continues to further climb the ramp, through its shadows. He then settles down to watch the studio floor—now milling with technicians who are setting up lights for a shot. The heaviness of his look is the weight of life and a loss rekindled specifically in this space and in the presence of the labour that is film-making. Both his identification with the crew as fellow-artists or fellow-technicians is also a dis-identification for he is not recognised. In fact, he is not even seen. The camera moves closer to the director's face that undulates as though it were an image in a pond disturbed by a pebble and the pebble in the pond does indeed become the succeeding image that quickly dissolves (this is reminiscent of the opening scene of *Pyaasa*). The director's face is now frozen as several moving 'studio images'—props, lights, camera, projector, applauding hands and autograph-seeking young women—are superimposed on his anguished expression. The adulation of the women becomes the cue for the analepsis and the next image is from another time, for the director is now shown leaning over the balcony of a movie theatre. He is younger, dressed in a dark well-cut suit smoking a pipe and gazing at the crowds coming to see his movie. In the next frame, the viewer is directly in the line of the director's gaze, as though part of the audience that has come to see his latest production and looking up at him as the façade of the theatre forms his backdrop—a reference to Orson Welles' *Citizen Kane*. Here is a new kind of extreme verticality, different from what we have experienced thus far—this is a verticality that grants stature and gives a sense of the fall that is always a risk for the famous. The studio metaphor has extended itself from production (film set) to the finished product (screening hall). What unites both process and product is the necessity of a collectivity—the collective labour that makes film and the collectivity that applauds or denigrates in the cinema hall.

The thematic and visual possibilities of these human bodies in confined spaces are effectively used in both the films and take on metaphoric force. In *Pyaasa*, the crowd or audience (apparently of poetry lovers) are initially faceless, still silhouettes but demonstrate how their herd-like thinking can easily turn from collective cheering to mob violence and stampede. In *Kaagaz ke Phool,* the crowds are film-going audiences and they easily turn into legions of fans begging for autographs and jostling to be around the celebrity. It is their enthusiastic applause that anoints the director and Shanti's first film together as a runaway success. For the director, eagerly awaiting the verdict of the collectivities of viewers, the meta-gaze (looking at film being looked at) carries the highest stakes. Later, the same collective (even if comprising of another set of individuals) will angrily reject the same director's artistic output, breaking chairs in the theatre, throwing footwear and creating mayhem.

Just as the roused mob is the necessary contrast to the suffering individual, the director's mastery over the studio space (a space that needs so many bodies that one is rarely physically alone) is contrasted by his fortress-like picturesque home that houses his vulnerability. Again borrowing from Welles, this Xanadu-like space carries props of emptiness, fluttering curtains, a clutter of statues (set-like in doing so, especially the large Buddha-head), wide walls with French windows, empty spaces and chessboard floors of light and dark. As with the sled called Rosebud in *Citizen Kane*, this is the setting to plant a metaphor of deepest longing and loss. While Kane may have longed for his own childhood, the director here craves to be a part of his daughter's childhood. The object representing this is revealed rather dramatically—the camera is inside a closed cupboard that the director opens to reach out to a shape in the foreground. The viewer is fleetingly admitted into the director's inner world—his hands pull out a doll, caress it and put it back in the cupboard. The soundtrack returns to the melancholic refrain of the opening sequence. The mood is broken only when the camera glides past the director and dissolves into another structure, a boarding school where he goes to meet his daughter.

The film will end with a return to the densely semanticised studio space for a last encounter between the director and Shanti. They are both acting in a scene (he becomes an 'extra' for money) but she does not recognise him. It is only as he is walking away and a studio hand pulls away his shawl that she notices him wearing a tattered sweater that was knitted and gifted by her. As she chases after him, we are returned to the outdoors—the studio lot from the opening visuals of the film. A strong wind is blowing as they both run and pieces of paper and a hurrying crew pass their way. Their run is against the force of the wind, the two bodies fighting destiny. They are finally separated at the gate of the studio, for she is mobbed by fans, unable to extricate herself and he, now one of the faceless unknown, runs alone into the stormy world. The visual imaging of the multitudes is essential to both films in so far as they are used to offset the profound separateness of solitary individual talent and desire—they become the screen, so to say, against which ambition and its downfall will be projected. The couple's belonging and exile from their shared creative and emotional space (that they can neither denounce nor embrace) is literal and physical and the crowds (the collectivity) represent this as much as the looming studio gate.

Not surprisingly, the studio is the site of the director's death. The outermost time frame of the film (the initial shots of the unkempt director walking up the ramp) turns out to be the last hours of his life. His death is the concluding scene of the film. Just as there was a constant ascent in the opening sequence (a figure climbing, the camera looking up), now we have a corresponding sequence of descent as the old director climbs down to the studio floor, lovingly touching the camera and settling down into the director's chair. The crew comes later to find that he is dead in the chair. But there is nobody to truly grieve for a man who has been forgotten by the industry that he worked for. Someone walks over and asks for the corpse to be taken away so that the scheduled shooting can be completed. As the men crowd around the dead director, the camera slowly travels up and looks to the ramp where the lights have come on, because, as had just been instructed, the day's shooting schedule has to begin.

Pacing the Sequence

The partnership of Guru Dutt and V.K. Murthy (as recounted in Kabir's biography of Guru Dutt and Rao's biography of Murthy) was an unusual churn of chaos and fastidiousness, a key factor in the visual pacing and atmosphere of their films. For instance, the visualisation of the seductive song *Jaane kya tune kahi, jaane kya maine suni* (Who knows what you said, who knows what I heard) in

Pyaasa is a strong demonstration of the aesthetic possibilities that an attentive and nimble camera eye can articulate. The song introduces the female protagonist on screen for the first time—the sex-worker Gulab who is soliciting customers in the city's nightscape and chances upon Vijay the poet. Typical of several such 'introductory moments' of stars on screen, the 'reveal' of the actress is delayed—the screen is filled by a mid-close shot of the back of her head veiled in a diaphanous white sari, luminously lit up against the night sky (Fig. 7). It is an ethereal look that cannot translate into colour and only the high tone of the black and white makes possible her acting as presencing. The viewer is aware of occupying the same gazing space as the poet on the bench—the gentle opening couplet of Gulab's song builds anticipation. The poet gets up from his bench and bends into a frame that focuses on Gulab, the backdrop speckled with light. As the poet calls out to her she turns to him and the viewer (Fig. 8). The poet's interjection—*Maine kaha* (I said...)—becomes the cue for her song (Who knows what you said…) and simultaneously a cue for the camera to spring into movement.

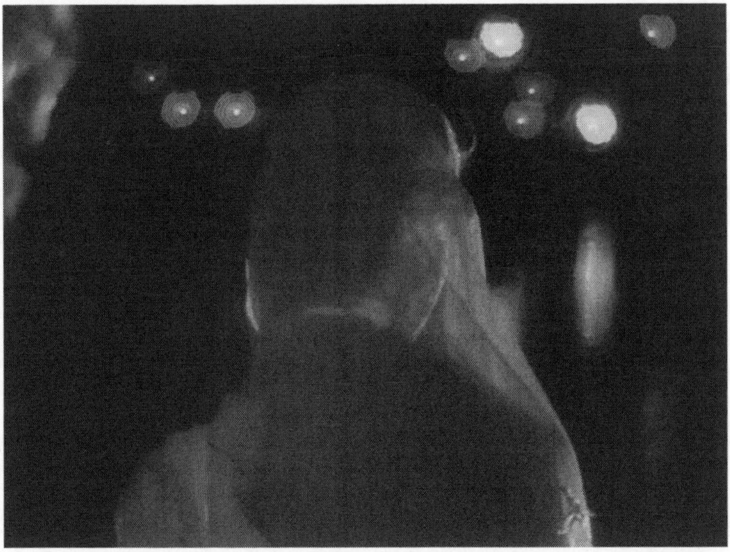

Fig. 7 *Source NFAI*

Fig. 8 Source NFAI

The camera keeps pace with both the movement of the song and the gait of the woman who will lead her potential customer into the promise of the night. Gulab's suggestive eyes and coquettish face fill up the frame as she glides with the gentle refrain of the song, the camera swaying with her, the telephoto lens blurring the city lights into flashes of temptation. The following frame pulls back and down to give Gulab the advantage and power of her seductive gaze. The spell remains unbroken in its exquisite fluidity as she shimmers back and through an arch, both the poet and the camera now completely mesmerised, entirely in synch with her. Gulab never looks into the lens—the viewer is a voyeur in this hypnotic space. Her gaze is always a little above the camera. The poet's reaction shots are far and few in between. The main romance here is between Gulab and the camera that mimics the presence of the poet but not his affect—the camera is eager and desirous unlike him, it plays the appreciator even as he remains ascetic. The camera follows him following her, her face always just moving into and catching the frame. There is a sense of just the two of them alone in a camera-determined private fascination. Murthy describes Guru Dutt's penchant for combining close-ups in 75 mm lens with choreographed movement (unconventional at that time) that made specific demands on the cinematographer with both lighting and composition.[13] Since the filming was not done on a reflex camera, the cinematographer could not rely on its viewfinder and the moving close-ups made it difficult to give 'fill in light' for shadows would shift constantly. Murthy improvised by clipping on a 100w or 200w bulb to the Mitchell camera and connecting it to a dimmer.[14] While Murthy does not specify which films or scenes made use of this particular technique, it is clear that between the aesthetic formulations of the director and the technical improvisations by the cinematographer, new innovations were emerging in the image-track. We mention this because of the particular treatment of the song being discussed, its combination of close-up and movement, the darting subject beautifully lit even while the frame retains specks of light in the enveloping darkness of the outdoor.

As Gulab continues to sing the song, in frame after frame, the camera clings to her—close shots highlight the dark of the night and the luminescence of her face. In a series of mid-close frames of her lit face and shoulders, the camera lens and angles vary slightly but perceptibly—these gently shifting proportions and positionings on the screen heighten the feeling of intoxication and disorientation. The song opens up to a wider shot of several large white columns. As Gulab runs, the camera playfully tracks along with her. 'The vertical columns that regularly break the horizontal movement of the camera create a visual rhythm that counterpoints and plays around with the rhythm of editing'.[15] The deliberate tilting of frames, moving as if off-kilter from the excitement of the seduction, change perspective but the camera is reluctant to look away from Gulab, reluctant to show us the city and just about manages to keep the poet in our consciousness (more as a following body than responsive face). Even though the city is suggested only through a few props—the benches, the streetlights, the columns and car headlights—a world is conjured. Soon the colonial building is replaced by narrowing lanes, Gulab still luring the poet and camera, her body sinuously darting across a lane. Her face and the shifting shape of its shadow glide along bleached cement walls (Fig. 9). The song ends with their reaching Gulab's house. The poet follows her, not as a seduced lover but in search of poetry—for he has identified the lyrics of her song as taken from a lost folio of his poetry.

Fig. 9 *Source NFAI*

The film is particularly adept at handling the question of desire through poetry. While Gulab's desire for the poet is first manifest through her adoption of his discarded folio by setting it to tune and voice, the poet's desires are barricaded, partly by the unrequited love for his college sweetheart and largely by his angst about the unfeeling nature of the world towards his art. One of the sequences that blend these two frames of desire is the pacing of one of the film's most evocative songs—*Aaj sajan mohe anjg lagalo* (Today my beloved, hold me in your embrace). The lyrics of the song draw from the Baul Vaishnava tradition, whereby the deity is imagined as a passionate lover. Here, the song is visualised as two parallel planes—in one, a woman devotee is singing to God on a city pavement and in the other, there is Gulab who aches to express her love for the poet but is perhaps held back by the fear of being misunderstood. The poet has just rescued Gulab from harassment by a policeman by calling her his wife—a legitimacy that touches her. In the song, the dark synthetic sari of the intensely listening sex-worker makes a sharp contrast to the coarse white robes of the devotee singing of/in abandon. They are of course both devotees, both given to passionate devotion, the spiritual and the sensual strung together as one. As Vasudevan has noted: 'The relatively stable articulation of these three points in the narrative construction—devotional voice, desiring woman, and her object—effects a dynamic temporal deployment…'.[16] The frames alternate between close-ups of these two faces of desire—the evenly lit face of the devotee and the shaded face of the sex-worker that is framed with fabric and loose locks of hair. An extreme close-up of Gulab's face follows—this time her gaze slowly rising to the top of the stairs where the poet has gone. Tears line her eyes. The slow-moving portraiture, showcasing the desire-laden eyes of both women, is the spark before the fruition. As the song unfurls, Gulab staggers to the stairs, the lyrics of the song settling in her mind. Her slow walk to the music of the song is extended—the two flights of stairs are made to seem much higher, the camera staying close to Gulab in the move upward.

The first shot of the terrace is a point of view of Gulab—it fully inhabits her physical movement and the anxiety embedded in her heart. The frame starts with a glimpse of open space (sky, terrace), and although this is a relief after the enclosed stairway, the space feels forlorn without the beloved that Gulab seeks. The camera pans to the right (her anxiety skillfully captured in its tempo) to catch a glimpse of the poet. He is standing at the edge of the terrace, leaning against the parapet, cigarette in hand, looking down at the singer on the street. His white clothes mirror that of the singer, the light of the street on his face, the wind and light sculpting and outlining his legs. The unspoken desire in Gulab can only watch him from her niche in the shadows of the terrace—desire pinions his figure. The song makes the space of the terrace seem expansive—it suggests an elasticity of space, and the space-time of the song allows a further stretching of desire. To Gulab's half-shut eyes, the poet is near yet so far in the dark space of that small, empty terrace, her eyes on him, his on the city below. There is pure desire and unbridgeable distance, and they remain in two distinct and untouching solitudes.

Fig 10 *Source NFAI*

The camera rises, the ambience turns darker, more night-like, increasingly empathetic to Gulab's stirring (Fig 10). The weight of the moment is entirely in her facial expressions (*abhinaya*). As the song progresses Gulab comes closer and closer to the poet, eyes brimming with tears, and leans ahead, as if to touch him, almost does so, but changes her mind, withdraws and runs away. That moment of the inability of touch is not a moralising moment, or even of the oscillation between avowal and renunciation, but rather a moment of the sequence reaching its climax. All the frames of desire—the two women and the oblivious man—collapse into visual fruition. Her flight from him at the end of the song is not a negation but rather yokes them together in the space of the frame visually and absolutely. The consummation that the narrative arc of the film will not permit (the mortal singer on the street seeking the immortal, the sex-worker lusting for the upright poet) is actuated and experienced through the astute and sensitive visual pacing of the scene.

The determination to put visual language to work where the spoken cannot reach, or is destined to be inadequate and might fail is a repeated preoccupation with Guru Dutt. The elisions of language are too wide, too inaccessible, especially when the situation involves a mating that would be considered morally inappropriate though perfectly organic to the two people in love. The cinematic treatment of music and pacing similar to the one between the poet and Gulab discussed previously also takes place in *Kaagaz ke Phool*. Here, the director is a married man (with a teenage daughter) and is aware of the growing attraction between him and Shanti, the female protagonist of the film. The first full enunciation of their desire again happens in and through a song. This song like the devotional/erotic song discussed earlier is sung in the same intoxicative style by Geeta Dutt—*Waqt ne kiya kya haseen sitam* (Time has wrought such exquisite injustice). However, unlike the Baul singer's rendition, this is a slow plaintive number with no percussion and the setting is the flat floor of the studio (unlike the multiple spatialities of stairs, terrace and street in the earlier song in *Pyaasa*). A brief interaction between the couple precedes the song. The scene starts with a shot that is regularly repeated in the film (and immediately signals emotional intensity to the viewer)—this is a top angle wide frame of a dark studio floor, the director walking in through a brightly lit doorway, his shadow filling up a large part of the frame. There is another figure in the frame—Shanti is sitting on a chair but she is so lost in the shadows that, like him, the viewer too does not quite notice her. The lighting has created three affective planes for the viewer—(a) the set of the film-within-film which has a white (blank) screen that the characters and the viewers face, (b) the bright light falling on the director who sits on his chair with his back to us and (c) the shadows around the chair that Shanti occupies. This last is the plane closest to the camera. Placed against the white screen that the director is gazing intently are lights on their stands like heads on spines, evoking frozen actors. The camera starts to track back to reveal Shanti in her chair (Fig. 11). Her knitting needle drops and the director turns around at this aural cue. The visual spell is broken. A conversation ensues and their mutual attraction becomes evident. He tells her that he is married and has a family. She knows it of course but loves him nonetheless. Instrumental music starts to play as the wide theatrical shot is re-established as he walks away from her. Light bathes her from the door and the camera slowly starts to rise. The song by a disembodied, non-synched female voice is about the exquisite pain inflicted by time, a pain and longing magnified by the clutter of the studio space with shadows that the camera slowly moves in and out of. Through the song, lights turn off and on to reveal unexpected depths and interiors. The camera tracks as a penetrative desire—likewise, it can track back as recoil, disillusionment—as it sweeps across patterns on the floor, shadows in foreground, low looming ceilings, stretches of wall. Each shot is unhurried and takes its time—the longer the take there is a greater sense of a real-world depth and the cramping and uncramping of compositional space. As the opening lyrics end, the strings pick-up tempo and the camera tracks swiftly across the studio floor, the two characters now small and distant. The skylight opens just then and a dazzling shaft of light drops down, a visual cue for the unattainability of desire (Fig. 12). A vast space opens up within the studio and then shuts.

Fig. 11 *Source NFAI*

Fig. 12 *Source NFAI*

In the four shots that follow, where the camera alternates between their two expressions, moving from over the shoulder of one character towards the face of the other, the earlier shaft of light is strangely missing. Soon after, the wide shot returns with the diagonal light but this time it makes no attempt at realism, for there are now four figures on the screen—the director and his love are frozen in their social/emotional limitations as well as in their physical distances in the frame. The other two figures are ghostly apparitions of the pair (lit, shadow selves) that start to move towards each other, towards the centre of the screen and into the pillar of light where they can finally meet. Their faces project their hunger for each other. Shanti moves closer to the director as the camera circles in sympathy but the proximity cannot be sustained and she has to walk away from him into the depths of the studio. The diagonal shaft of light has again disappeared and we are returned to the steady light from the doorway.

V.K. Murthy describes the inclusion of this shaft of light—the pains he took for the lighting is recounted at length in his biography, from which the following narrative has been taken.[17] Guru Dutt and he were sitting outside Mehboob Studio (in Bombay) when they saw sunlight streaming in through a ventilator, with the dust of the studio making it more dramatic. They decided to recreate the effect for the film. Murthy tried to use a focus spot lens on the light but the light felt too diffused, more like a divergent beam than the even and parallel beam that the sunlight had created for them earlier. The solution to this occurred to Murthy a few days later when he saw a make-up man walk past with a mirror that reflected light on the wall. The production team was asked to procure two mirrors of about 4 by 3 feet. One mirror was made to face the sun while the other mirror was put on the studio catwalk. The light reflecting off the first mirror fell on the second mirror and made it possible for Murthy to manipulate the beam as he wished. In addition, he used dust and smoke to make the shaft of light more prominent. This effect was used twice in the film—once for the song just discussed and later when the director dies.

The director's death at the end is part of the strong intertextuality that *Kaagaz ke Phool* creates with the story of *Devdas*. The widely filmed and influential story of Devdas—his dying for socially unsanctioned love had become part of the ethos of Indian cinema—was coincidentally the film that the director Suresh was shooting. In the last chapter of *Devdas*, the protagonist travels in a cart to the house of his childhood love but dies before they meet. In the song being discussed in *Kaagaz ke Phool* (*Waqt ne kiya*…), the prop of the cart serves as the frame-within-the-frame. The director leans against the cart, his back to the camera, as his love awaits him at the far end of the studio, centrally framed. The unconsummation of that relationship hangs heavy in the atmosphere of the studio. For much of the song, the characters continue to be anchored to the studio floor, the camera emoting their distress and helplessness, tracking in and out as if beseeching them to act on their passion. This projection is strongest in the last frame of the song, a wide shot again, the camera slowly moving up on the crane as the director resolutely walks towards his beloved in the distant chair. Will he embrace and acknowledge her love? But before he completes the stride and before he can step into the light from the doorway, the camera slows in anticipation and the frame slowly dissolves into black. It is a question that remains unanswered.

The Disappearing Greys

The settings of the most impactful and central scenes in both films are the morphing dark spaces—the auditorium in *Pyaasa* and the studio in *Kaagaz ke Phool.* Faces float in light and silence, appearing and dissolving in slivers of darkness. Light creates a time within, a pooling of the seconds that accumulate as in a silent film. The songs we hear in these spaces sometimes speak against silence and are also absorbed into their greater silence. Lovers cannot articulate their love or anguish—it is a stylised silence. Cinema is rarely as powerful as in that pulsing moment of the large, empty space of the studio, pregnant with a million scenes—and yet, for now, bare, emptied and transitory. The darkness of the early morning or the late evening is not inert darkness but a steadily growing volume. Often, there may be no immediate tragedy in the plot but there is much pathos that works through the contrast of black and white. An example can be given from *Pyaasa*. As the poet leaves the publisher's office and encounters his college sweetheart (now married to the owner of the publishing house) in the elevator of the building, the shot starts with the pulling back of iron shutters (of the old elevator) as if he were entering jail, the lighting stark—a band of black covering the top half of his face. The elevator fills with people but the lighting indicates that the two are only conscious of each other—the wall of the elevator is so dark that it becomes a screen on which a shimmering blurred face mysteriously appears and transitions to a memory. In a few quick strokes and poignant use of dark patches, an inscape and a past have been educed.

V.K. Murthy is on record saying that *Pyaasa* was his favourite film.[18] He explains the chances he was able to take with exposing film to very low light readings:

> I had studied photography. I knew what intensity was, what illumination meant. For every film speed if certain foot-candles [light exposure] are used, the image will satisfactorily emerge. Suppose 100 foot-candles are needed to get a first class [film] negative, and let's assume it will tolerate 200 foot-candles on the higher intensity side and 35 foot-candles on the under side—I would decide the kind of results I wanted and at times would go as low as 20 foot-candles! Not many people had this courage. It is because I had studied. I had properly understood and applied the specifications that were given with the film, that's all.[19]

This technical choice explains several frames in both the films that feel like they have barely enough light for the human eye to see and for the silver nitrates on the film to register. This is even as they remain fully imagined worlds with all kinds of real and implied detailing. The camera becomes a lighting pen. At times, even when the scene is not underexposed or swathed in darkness, the sense of contrast remains in the lighting and exposure.

One of the central scenes in *Pyaasa* is when the poet is hired by the publisher and invited to his house to help out with a party he is hosting with this wife—by now the viewer understands that this is the publisher's way of confirming his suspicion of the past romantic dalliance between his wife and the poet. The gathering comprises several poets and we are told that some of them are the greatest poets of the age. But the 'real poet' or rather the one with whom our sympathies have been anchored is there only to be publically humiliated, made to work as a waiter and domestic help. The popular song *Jaane woh kaise log the* (Who knows what sort of people…) begins soon after the established poets have recited their ornate traditional courtship poetry and received appreciation. In contrast, the 'real poet' starts to recite thoughts about (un)requited love in a fluid and colloquial 'modern' idiom. The first line starts and stops—the camera shows no interest in moving away from its wide shot of the room and all the guests, even though the singer (poet) is not part of the frame. An older poet encourages the young man to continue. The shot begins with a close-up of the poet, his gaze averted, a line of dark hardbound books behind him. His clothes are bleached white in contrast with the dark shadow his head casts on the books. As he starts to look up and continue the song, the frame starts to open and expand until we recognise the leitmotif of the film—the silhouetted man with outstretched arms. The poet is dressed entirely in a white drape, unlike the previous shabby overcoat—this is the occasion of his 'reemergence' after the alumni meet. The evenly lit dazzling white shirt and shawl claim full space and he likewise claims a higher moral ground. This is reaffirmed when the woman he loves is dressed in black and repeatedly shown leaning against a white wall.

At the heart of the poetry that Sahir Ludhianvi brings to *Pyaasa* is a compelling conviction in the power of writing to bear witness and speak against the discriminations and hierarchies of the social order. In another plaintive composition later in the film that is more recited than sung—the refrain is *Jinhe naaz hai hind par woh kahan hai* (Where are the people who have pride in India?)—the poet becomes the conscience of a decrepit moral world. This song is an adaptation of a poem that Sahir Ludhianvi had written in college called *Chakle* (Brothels) and begins with the lines—*Ye kooche ye neelam ghar dilkashi ke* (These lanes, the auction-houses of pleasure). These have been appreciated for being a 'fine example of political comment combined with humanitarian compassion'.[20] The disillusionment of the jaded independence (of 1947) is captured in a sequence of shots arranged like a tableau. Each frame is a complete story that is aligned with the lines sung. It is an excellent example of how the affect of a song is created equally by the lyric and the visual, not as complementary but as composite. This sequence has been created in the language of black and white stills by a camera obsessed with shadows. Unlike most of the songs picturised by Guru Dutt and V.K. Murthy, where the fluidity of theme and visual treatment is a priority, this song has to be deliberately understood as a series of staccato expressions—brief and pointed. The setting is the red light area where the poet has just stepped away from a performance by a woman forced to dance while her child is ill. The poet is the exiled participant-observer of this liminal space of social (dis)reputation and the transactions of body and pleasure.

The opening tune begins with an extreme close-up of the poet's face in profile—patches of light fall on his nose, eye and cheek. The play of black and white is established for the rest of the song. The next shot is a tilt down from a lit window, a pan across a pitch-black wall to the silhouettes of women looking down at the bright lights of the street. We return to the poet who is still humming the opening bars of his song, a white glass of intoxicant held against his face—perhaps a cultural reference to the literary/film character Devdas who is associated in public imagination with courtesans, alcoholism and the great disillusionment of love. Walking through the streets, reciting poetry that is simultaneously moral commentary, holding his glass up to clear view, the poet becomes an anti-Devdas, the truth-bearer of a generation, rather than one drowning in purely personal angst. The camera in this sequence retains the staccato effect by periodically returning to freeze the protagonist's face at close quarters. The freezing is not literal pausing of action but the sustenance of strong facial expression. And even though the effect of the outdoors is meant to be gritty, the setting is dreamlike—patches of the street are over-lit and the poet is surrounded by tall windows and window-bars. Even as he sways through the streets the clinging camera unsteadily following him—all other faces are silhouettes or blurred, inconsequential. The light is dramatic as if it is an inner light and space, allegorical—huddled, shamed figurines, a sordidness, the helpless, exhausted gait of the many walking up and down those same streets that they are doomed to never transcend. His face is half-lit or in profile or three quarters, while theirs is always in shadow, diseased, obscured by arches, subject to fleeting violence, unindividuated.

The conflict caused by art (lack of recognition, destitution and exploitation) can only be resolved through art—through poetry that can decry, denounce and win 'posthumous' (he is believed to be dead) acclaim. He can then renounce that belated materialistic fame and claim a new moral vantage. Among the last scenes of *Pyaasa* is a visual representation of this moral positioning—it is one of the most memorable black and white scenes in Indian cinema, a conscious use of the absence of greys, with the dominance of black and white used to underline the axis of right and wrong. The scene takes place on a public platform, specifically the proscenium stage—another similarity that *Pyaasa* has with *Aag*. The preceding moment, as with *Aag*, is the milling of the crowds to the towering walls of the auditorium past large gateways and doorways—collectivist humanity is dwarfed and massified. The first frame inside the auditorium is an extraordinary manipulation of several vertical and horizontal planes. In the foreground of the frame are passive silhouettes of men seated in auditorium chairs—the camera's eye is lowered to the level of the row closest to it. At the centre is a brightly lit archway through which a figure clothed half in black (shawl) and half in white (*dhoti*) is walking to the centre of the screen. Even though we are yet to see the proscenium stage, it is established that this space at the very last row of the audience is the 'real' stage where the 'real' hero stands and where the action will happen—for the conventional proscenium is now revealed to be a sham, dotted with insincere people commemorating the false death of a poet. The triumph of this cinematic moment is its complete embrace of the power of contrasts. The greys are muted—the rest of the scene tries to sustain this effect through sharp pockets of light. The following frame shows the grandeur of the stage—the chandeliers, the carvings, the expanse of space from wall to wall, from floor to ceiling. Even as the music builds in crescendo, four images of the stage in progressive focal lengths appear consecutively. These function as sharp cut-ins to the wider setting of the drama till it reaches the central figure of the publisher—the four shots have a collective screen time of only nine seconds. Behind the publisher is a veiled statue. As the viewer's mind and eye, caught in the pattern of moving ahead to the centre, expects a further close-up of the editor or the veiled statue, the next frame brilliantly overturns the anticipation with a close-up of the poet at the back of the auditorium again reminding us where the affective action lies. It is as if the statue behind has been unveiled to reveal the poet's face.

The editor starts to speak and the images alternate between the grandeur of the stage (as also the speech) and the incredulous disturbed expressions on the listening poet's face, his face sharply lit—one half in shadow, the other in light. As the poet staggers and leans against a wall, the camera's relation to his face is greater than the volubility of the editor. The poet's tremulous singing (which begins just then) is the answer to that banal volubility. The poet stretches his arms to a stance seen before (against the bookshelf in the party). But this time the confined and private space of the employer's library has been replaced by an exposed public stage. In the first frame of the poet's stance, the black wall is continuous with the unlit blackness of one arm and the other side of his face and crumpled shirtsleeve catch the light. V.K. Murthy cites the parameters of realism to light the hero thus despite numerous objections by his contemporaries—to him, it was intuitive that a man looking inside a dark auditorium would have very little light on his face.[21] This effect (of backlighting and dark frontality) is retained as the camera reframes the poet as a full-figure in a mid shot that will quickly pull into a wider shot that can accommodate the audience. The dimly lit men in the hall have to turn around (or peer from the balcony) to look at this 'real' action (Fig. 13).

Fig. 13 Source NFAI

Even in this public, the poet remains self-absorbed, introspective, even when singing aloud—*Yeh duniya agar mil bhi jaaye toh kya hai* (Even if I find [fame in] this world, it would not matter). The audience is passive, respectful, standing up and listening. The people on the stage have recognised the poet but the only true response (for it is one of gratitude and joy that he is alive) belongs to Gulab who is dressed entirely in dark fabric—her head lightly covered by the fabric like a grieving Madonna. Through the song, the poet remains mostly lit from behind by the bright light beyond the archway till two henchmen of the publisher pick him up and carry him out by force. The crowd heaves and the camera moves with them, the light around the poet is bleached. In the succeeding frames, the poet jostles in light and shadow, pulling ahead with anguished determination as several arms holding him drag him back. The repetition of the action from several angles adds to the general disorientation of the melee. He is singing his rejection of the world's hypocrisy—*Jala do, jala do* (burn it, burn it). He is turned into a performer and an unexpected vitality courses through him when the lights are suddenly turned off by the publisher—Gulab is injured in the ensuing stampede. A foot comes down on her just as it had on the bee in the opening scene of the film where the poetry was delicate and wistful, farthest away from this present outburst of rage and pain. The chaos of the agitated audience again brings back references to the inferno in the theatre during the finale of *Aag*.

In a doubling that allows the poet a chance to properly address (then decry) his audience, the auditorium scene is repeated. The poet is brought back to the public gaze to be honoured for his work. This time he is on the proscenium stage united with the microphone that was on stage with him during the scene of the alumni meet. The lighting of the scene, the auditorium and the stage is exactly the same as previously discussed but this time the concluding chaos is more violent and the poet is reduced to tattered clothes. The contrast here is between a hero and a crowd, one incomplete without the other, whether to seek validation or rejection. To be heroic is to surrender the very identity of the heroic (as a social, public figure). The poet walks away from the fame, denouncing it as hollow, but takes Gulab with him. The last frame of the film is of two silhouettes walking away from the camera towards a bright horizon. Guru Dutt had intended for the film to end with the poet leaving alone but was persuaded to add the companion when distributors protested.[22] The resolution as a flight from the world is repeated at the end of *Kaagaz ke Phool*, although the literal running away (of the director) is from love and the possibility of social rehabilitation, infusing it with melancholia and pessimism that perhaps affected the film's box office reception.

As with *Pyaasa*, the first meeting of the artist and his future-muse in *Kaagaz ke Phool* takes place in the city at night—the openness of the spaces gives the encounter of strangers a clear legitimacy but the cover of the dark also gives them privacy that would otherwise be missing in public spaces. The mood is further heightened by rain and wind as Suresh rushes to take cover under a tree and finds a young woman already there. The use of contrasts can be seen in the setting—the tree and Suresh in black as also the river in the background, while the drenched woman and the lights of the city are white. A conversation follows about the weather and the ways of 'gentlemen who cannot be trusted'. However, Suresh insists that he is indeed a gentleman who can be trusted and lends her his overcoat. Their conversation and cinematic framing have to work within the few shards of light that night allows. The exchange about the coat (how a cold is free but a coat is not, implying her economic straits) is the reason for the two to meet again in Bombay—she has to return his coat. The scene is equally important for the meeting of black with white because the moment that his dark coat comes around her light sari is the moment that shapes their affinity.

Shanti and the director meet again in the studios of Bombay—it turns out that he is looking for a 'fresh face' to play the role of Paro the village belle in his production of *Devdas*. He asks for Shanti to be dressed for the part (with costume and make-up)—for the third time the director and his muse meet (the first time being the storm and the second being her sudden entry on the set as described in the opening pages of this book). This third meeting will also be a play of contrasts, of black and white that eschews the grays. The setting for this meeting is theatrical—the crowds of the studio set (technicians) are all gone and the frame is wide, as if on a theatre stage. The director walks into the frame (away from the camera, now the 'fourth wall') towards his chair and settles in. The most striking thing about the frame is the single diagonal spotlight that cuts across the screen. The next frame is equally wide but much darker, poised for the entry of the director's muse. Shanti stands at the lit doorway, destined for the spotlight that awaits her—she walks past it and towards him (Fig. 14). The attention of the frame remains with her as evinced by the succeeding frames. It is only in the slant of light that he can truly recognise and baptise her as the character she has to play on screen. Their bond has been visually cemented by the lights of the studio.

Fig. 14 *Source NFAI*

The last meeting between the director and Shanti mirrors the black-white pattern of their first meeting, but this time in the glare of the studio lights. They are part of a scene-within-a-scene. She is on the social ascendant, a film star dressed again in white—but it is the white of renunciation (a Meera-like devotee figure). He is huddled on the floor in a dark shawl acting the part of a destitute man that indeed mirrors his current social standing. The visual binary that indicates their divergent destinies is pre-determined—it is black and white that can never merge into grey.

V.K. Murthy won his first Filmfare award (for cinematography) for *Kaagaz ke Phool*. Murthy recalls that during an argument between him and Guru Dutt on an earlier film about Murthy's perfectionism (and consequently, the setting-up time) that he demanded, Guru Dutt had asked him to settle for now. He promised that one day he would make a film *for* Murthy. This would be *Kaagaz ke Phool* where he told Murthy to take as much time as he wished with lighting to get the images he wanted.[23] The heightened visuality of the film was able to claim both gritty realism as well as a stylised abstraction and allegorical quality. Arun Khopkar comments on the changes in the aperture during shots (in *Kaagaz ke Phool*), 'altering the ratio of light and shade on a face and extricating an image from the chain of cause and effect that binds realism'.[24] The partnership of Guru Dutt and V.K. Murthy that actualised such innovations was a partnership of deep creative camaraderie and the rejection of the film by contemporary viewers was a blow to both. There are several accounts of people throwing footwear at the screen during the premier of the film. It was a humiliation that would greatly affect both of them—Murthy wonders if his photography eclipsed the storyline. At any rate, Guru Dutt never directed a film again.[25]

After Guru Dutt's death, Govind Nihalani who worked as Murthy's assistant recalls asking Murthy how he felt when Guru Dutt died. Murthy said, 'You know, I did not cry for him, I cried for myself'.[26] Nihalani speculates on this pithy response.

> This sentence summed up their entire relationship. He felt it was the end of his art, his craft. He knew that in the future it would not be easy to get opportunities to do the work he had done so far. An age had ended for him. A new age was starting.[27]

Murthy dwells repeatedly on the tumultuous love-hate relationship he had with Guru Dutt, their many fights, their great friendship and it is clear that the dynamics of their personalities shaped the aesthetics of the films they worked on together. Black and white cinema would in time forswear the extraordinary risks V.K. Murthy took with low-light exposures that supplemented the intensity of Guru Dutt's specific expertise in shooting songs—songs are the bejewelled islands at the centre of their craft. The meridian of this combined artistry, one of the finest examples of the black and white visual aesthetics of Hindi cinema, would also be the first directorial venture of Abrar Alvi, Guru Dutt's long-time screenplay and dialogue writer. This evocative journey into old-world hierarchies as well as forbidden passions and hidden torments—a triangulation of fraught relationships indicated in its very title, *Sahib Bibi Aur Ghulam* (Master, Mistress and Servant, 1962)—forms the last chapter of this book.

The Waiting Dissolve: Abrar Alvi's *Sahib Bibi aur Ghulam* (1962)

An adaptation of a Bengali novel written by Bimal Mitra in 1953, the plotline of *Sahib Bibi aur Ghulam* (Master, Mistress and Servant) is nested in the closing years of the nineteenth century and the early twentieth century.[1] In the literary imagination of the country, the *fin-de-siècle* is suffused with nostalgia for the passing of an older world, especially that of a desire that can exist in the public realm as creativity and sexuality.[2] The *tawaif* or the courtesan often became the placeholder of this nostalgia and longing—Miraz Hadi Ruswa's *Umrao Jaan Ada* (1899), adapted to film several times over the decades, is perhaps the most celebrated example. A recent discovery of his forgotten manuscript from the same year *Junun-e-Intezar* (The Madness of Waiting) reveals further layers to this yearning that is able to thrive because it comes to life between the lines that divide domesticity (and social respectability) vis-à-vis public exposure. This aestheticised 'madness of waiting' becomes the visual anchoring of *Sahib Bibi aur Ghulam*, one of the last films that Guru Dutt acted in and produced, having passed the directorial baton to his trusted associate Abrar Alvi (1927–2009). It was Guru Dutt's decision to buy the rights of the novel to make a Hindi–Urdu version of the film in consultation with the novelist.[3] The visual language composed by cinematographer V.K. Murthy is continuous with *Pyaasa and Kaagaz ke Phool* in its exploration of contrasts and the studied pacing of frames. Abrar Alvi also credits Guru Dutt with the direction of all the song sequences in the film[4]—this is significant as the visualisation of the songs is central to our analysis of *Sahib Bibi aur Ghulam*. Thus one is able to better appreciate the extension of the aesthetics from the films studied in the previous chapter. The visual orientation in

Sahib Bibi aur Ghulam is further extended to not just specific frames and movements but into a further affective dissolution of the many distances between the characters, with each type of distance and proximity captured in a distinct visual idiom. This is a camera that takes its time, waits in frames, sequences and transitions, to evoke that which is passing—it is a lulling of distance, heartbreak and tragedy that each character experiences in their own way.

The dissolve in cinema has traditionally referred to the overlapping of images—the fading in of one image and the fading out of another—and it frequently signifies the passage of time. As a narrative device, the dissolve has also served to negotiate transitions between several planes of storytelling and to show inscape or psychological shifts and mutations. In addition to these three elements—passage of time, plot transition, psychological overtone—the cinematic crafting in *Sahib Bibi aur Ghulam* invites one to think of dissolves as pause and waiting. The central focus of this chapter is the idea of dissolve as the overlap of two affective strands (of pause and waiting) that twine in one cinematic moment. This represents the aspiration of the film to negotiate disparate desires—especially those divided by gender, class, caste, circumstances and time. The aesthetic in the film thus evokes and celebrates a cinema of waiting, loss and unrequitement of a melancholia-in-itself. As Tarkovsky remarks: 'The artistic image is always a metonym, where one thing is substituted for the other, the smaller for the greater.'[5] To tell of what is living, the artist uses something dead; to speak of the infinite, she shows the finite. In *Sahib Bibi aur Ghulam*, the poignancy of the metonymic, finite image (such as the mansion or the marital bed) is infused with a non-consummatory quality. There is extended use of slow tracks, the starkness of light and dark, of suspended time— there is especially the reaction time within the shot. The camera is a waiting, anticipating camera, seeking to track with the characters' (unfulfillable) desire. More than any of the preceding chapters, the film is less the capturable still frame/photograph that emblematises the aesthetic and more the movement and sway of the camera. This is why it is necessary, to do justice to the film, to imagine the figures in this chapter as part of a movement that we have sliced and stilled only for analytic purposes. Further, this chapter reads the possibilities created by means of this swaying visual construction as it interfaces with the themes of waiting, lamenting, the incipient extinction of worlds and orders of things.

Sahib Bibi aur Ghulam invokes a waiting that cannot be abstract and is given the heft of bricks and of towering columns that are strong presences in both the opening and concluding scenes. The film is set at the end of the nineteenth century and anchored in the physical presence of a wealthy family home (a *haveli*). This grandiose *haveli* is not just the backdrop to the story of thwarted desires but seems rather a habitation for time itself. The youngest daughter-in-law of the *haveli,* Choti Bahu (the 'mistress' mentioned in the film's title, essayed by Meena Kumari) is willing to go to any lengths to win the heart and loyalty of her philandering aristocratic/landed husband (the 'master' in the title, played by Rehman) and in this, she recruits the help of a young educated man Bhootnath (the 'servant' in the title, played by Guru Dutt) who occupies a room in the outhouse of the *haveli.* Bhootnath brings for Choti Bahu a box of vermillion produced by the company he works for—it is a formulation that advertises aphrodisiac properties. When that does not secure her husband's affection and when told that her husband would rather be with someone who would sing and drink with him (like the courtesans he visits), Choti Bahu takes to alcohol and soon enough becomes dependent on it. Needless to say, her husband's attitude to her does not change. Her suffering is the central strand of the film—the film ends ineluctably with her violent death. Bhootnath continues in the story as the surviving mournful witness—the film opens and closes in a 'present-day' time frame while the rest of the story is told in analepsis. Returning to the *haveli* years later for a construction, he is shocked when the labourers on the site exhume Choti Bahu's skeletal hand with a gold bangle that he recognises with a start.

This chapter's analysis starts with Bhootnath's first sighting of Choti Bahu. In this instance, he sees her from a distance. She is seen entirely as shadow and as introverted vulnerability. Unaware of being watched, she is singing her pain from an interior, private room of the *haveli*. To Bhootnath and the viewer, she is a floating distant figurine, more a haunting aural refrain than a visual or physical being. The manner in which these distances and intimacies are visually imagined, executed and edited make this scene an ideal starting point for an exploration of the forms of dissolve that attempt to capture the sense of suspended time that is integral to the film.

An Image for Sound

The opening fifteen minutes of the film is entirely about preparing the viewer for the central dynamics of the story (that is the relationship between Choti Bahu and Bhootnath). This is in spite of their relationship being the most distant in terms of class and marital position. Bhootnath has heard about Choti Bahu from a faithful servant of the *haveli* (who happens to be related to him)—but he is yet to meet her. His anticipation is also ours—he looks out at the *haveli* and waits for the sight of her. His waiting can only ripen when it meets her waiting—for she too is waiting for her dissolute husband to come home after his nights of pleasure and indulgence at the *kothas* (homes of courtesans). The camera expertly dissolves these two waitings to create a visual horizon. Realistically, there are no circumstances that can make possible a direct easeful encounter between a married woman who lives in the *antarmahal* (inner chambers) of the *haveli* and an impoverished, visiting single man who is staying with the domestic help in the servant quarters. Even a fleeting sight would be unlikely. But what can travel across these barricaded social and visual spaces is sound and the achievement of the film is in turning aurality (her song) into a visual semiotic. This visuality enshrines and endorses Choti Bahu's patience with regard to the slow-passing of time—night after night she awaits her husband's return from his revelry. This is Choti Bahu's first appearance on screen. For Bhootnath, who does not know this tragic backstory, the sight of Choti Bahu is, initially, as a simple object of curiosity. The darkness of the *haveli* makes the viewer's gaze equally intrusive for the viewer too does not know the sorrowful context of her waiting. Though this is an intrusion into a married woman's private thoughts in the middle of the night, there is a delicacy and respect built into the grammar of the scene—a visual delicacy somewhat at odds with the prurience of Bhootnath and the audience. This delicacy is achieved through astute camera placements, lighting and the visual choreography of action.

The aural cue that triggers the scene is the call of bass strings that accompany a woman's voice that slowly sings of dousing the evening lamps (*Diya bhuja bhuja*). The melody is one of heartbreak—disembodied, faint, an externalisation of Bhootnath's increasing fascination with her spectral figure. It is his first dim awareness of Choti Bahu's pain. The reveal of Choti Bahu is gradual—the camera tries to delay it as long as possible. In this scene she is only a distant figure—there is only voice and song and no close-up. The effect of this is to highlight waiting and longing—sentiments integral to the film and which it tries to sustain throughout.

This is perhaps why even though the song emerges from her lips, the frame at the opening bar of the music is on the listener (Bhootnath)—someone who has heard of her but has never seen her. The listener is supine, hugging a pillow to his stomach. He sits up as the song starts. Outside, the guards are shown sleeping in their upright posture. An intimacy is thus established between his bare and humble lodgings and the grand interior of the house—the music flows past the sleeping guard. Two frames of the building follow—the first is a wide establishing shot of the *haveli* in the night with defined small blocks of light, a conspicuous fountain in the foreground and the second shot is a closer frame of the arched lit space of the *haveli*. The editing is unhurried. The music is still unlocated, its tempo as slow as the movement of the camera catching Bhootnath's sleepy wakefulness and careful movement. The song has hesitancy, silence, a throb—he stands up, coming outside to the verandah as if called gently. As the enunciation of the words of the first line becomes clearer, there is a close-up of his face—a seriousness to his face that the rustic-buffoon Bhootnath had not yet shown. The song starts to soar both in volume and mood, a hungry reaching out—when this happens, the camera itself starts to move. The slow track follows Bhootnath as he walks from within the room to the open corridor outside. He has turned from listener to viewer—the stretch of wooden railings between the camera and character gives way to a central framing of Bhootnath. The walls on either side of this character bear streaks of shadow, a sharp interspersing of light and dark that responds to the voice saying '*Chale aao, chale aao*' (come, come), as the character moves towards the camera (Fig. 1). This call defines the waiting of the scene.

Fig. 1 *Source NFAI*

Two parallel shots intercut—the first is a close-up of Bhootnath walking across the corridor, his face in and out of the shadow. The second is a track at the same pace (standing in for his point of view, although the angle of the gaze is not as frontal) of the *haveli*. Bhootnath continues to move through the corridor as though it were endless but both his walk and his gaze have to pause, for now, we will have the first visual presence of the singing woman. His point of view is the gait of a shadow on the top floor of the *haveli*—there is no lip-synch and yet we assume the shadow is the elusive singer. This haunted and haunting singer, stuck in some realm between life and death, evokes *Mahal* (discussed in the Overture of this book). The woman is now fully shown (in silhouette)—clearly, she is looking at the carriage and the song flows freely. The song is addressed in the familiar stylised mode to an absent beloved—and yet, there is no intended, embodied listener, except perhaps herself. The camera moves hastily towards Bhootnath, almost protective of him, anxious of his having crossed the limits of propriety (looking at a married woman in the night)—and as if in agreement with the anxious camera, Bhootnath looks away. The scene gathers momentum—a carriage brings the woman's husband home. Due to the conventions of Indian cinema, there is a sense of song emerging from the full body of the singing figure rather than lips or throat and the position of song-hearer cannot be located either as the camera freely triangulates her, Bhootnath and the arrivals from the carriage. There is a noticeable moment of affinity between the camera and Bhootnath: the latter bends into the shadows to get a better look at the drunk landlord being helped by his men and the next cut has the camera zoom in to a clear image of this action of helping. The camera thus gives the audience a view that Bhootnath cannot realistically have accessed. The woman's shadow then walks away, the song ends and Bhootnath is left to his thoughts—he continues to stand in the dark. The waiting has to continue and several more scenes intervene before Bhootnath has his first meeting with Choti Bahu.

It is important to note that this much-awaited encounter (that comes fifty minutes into the film) is also the first 'reveal' of the face of Choti Bahu. Her presence thus far has been aural and has loomed large in the psyche of the film as the key referent of Bhootnath's journey—his move from the stereotypical naivety of his provincial past to a more mature sense of tragic foreboding, the 'wisdom' of the present that includes domestic and romantic secrets. Bhootnath finds out soon enough (through the garrulous domestic help) that Choti Bahu's husband is following in the family tradition of husbands neglecting wives and spending all their time with mistresses and alcohol. To Bhootnath's mind, and to the viewer, Choti Bahu has become a larger-than-life tragic figure that one is irrepressibly drawn to. This feeling is exacerbated when the transgressive invitation to meet her finally arrives. Choti Bahu has asked for the unthinkable (in her social milieu) to meet a man unrelated to her in the *antarmahal* where both outsiders and men are forbidden. The only way this can happen is if Bhootnath is smuggled to the space—through the stairs at the back of the house, an ascent in darkness and shadows through a *haveli* that turns labyrinthine in the night. Will the waiting finally end—the scene is heightened by expectancy.

A nervous Bhootnath is pushed into a room (framed by tassels and draperies that indicate something delicate, veiled) by the domestic help who is then told to leave by Choti Bahu. Again, it is her voice that takes the lead and the visual is delayed even in this moment of reveal. The frame (sans her) is strongly filled with emotional anticipation—Bhootnath moves slowly into this forbidden space, alone, a frontal camera slowly tracking back in synch with his hesitant pace. The light is slanted and equally tentative with the dark spaces in the room that Bhootnath has to navigate. His eyes are fixed on the floor and the next frame embraces this point of view. The camera, the viewer and Bhootnath are fused in this move towards the first glance of the much-discussed and anticipated Choti Bahu. The chessboard floor of marble speaks of interior opulence. The camera looks down and slides over the floor as if the camera itself possessed hesitant footsteps. '*Aao*' (come) says Choti Bahu—the same call as the previous song. This beautifully choreographed shot is one of the most evocative and dynamic point-of-view experiences in Indian black and white cinema. The camera keeps its gaze steadily on the floor, brushes past curtains, reaches a patch where a woman's hand (clearly domestic help again) lays out a small carpet for sitting—an invitation to indicate that we (the viewer) are insiders, that we belong. The shot continues with its lowered 'floor gaze', the camera adroitly gliding on to a more lush tapestry till it reaches a woman's feet—decorated with jewelry and *alta* (red colouring), peeking out from behind a rich brocade sari (Fig. 2). '*Baitho*' (sit) says the Choti Bahu as the camera returns to an evenly lit frame of Bhootnath with downcast eyes and we get some sense that perhaps the previous point-of-view overshot its brief—that is, it glided over to see more than Bhootnath has seen thus far. This can be read as the agentiality of the camera inheriting the realist point of view but then moving even further into regions that the protagonist's eye has not yet accessed (this is similar to the earlier scene discussed when the husband returns at night). Bhootnath gently sits down, discomfort writ large. The camera, though independent of his averted gaze still does not dare look up at Choti Bahu's face—it continues to be awed and pans with her feet as she moves to another chair.

Fig. 2 *Source NFAI*

The camera then jumps the line of encounter, looking from behind her chair (she is suggested in the right foreground) and all attention is on Bhootnath's misery—his fingers twisting his dhoti, his body slumped, his brow furrowed. He explains his name to Choti Bahu—he was named Atulya Chakravarthy but has been called Bhootnath, a name that usually elicits laughter. Choti Bahu, however, does not laugh and praises the name—a surprised Bhootnath looks up. The close shot of his expression, almost like a child is matched (in scale) by the image that follows soon after—the waiting has ended and dissolved into the perfection of the visual tradition of portraiture. Choti Bahu is frozen in a pose, her hands overlapping below her chin, her sari draped on her head. The camera lovingly moves to her face—the portrait is choreographed and classical in presentation (Fig. 3). The light is even and diffused, making her seem luminous. The strains of a stringed instrument elevate the mood. Bhootnath is speechless—his close-up has none of the charge of the frame of Choti Bahu's face. An extreme close-up of this face follows—this time at the centre of the frame is her *bindi* (this is central to the plot because Bhootnath's task will be to fetch her supplies of vermillion that is alleged to have magical aphrodisiac properties). Two lights reflect like stars in her iris and Bhootnath is transfixed. The next extreme close-up is of her lips. The camera is deeply embedded in this moment, in her—both close-ups (of eyes and lips) delay the moment when the portrait will speak and discuss the ordinary minutiae of a wife's problems. As if suddenly reminded of his inappropriate stare, Bhootnath looks away. We return to the previous frame of the 'first look' and there is an animate quality to the portrait as she banters with affection.

Fig. 3 *Source NFAI*

In his reminiscences of the making of the film (with film journalist Satya Saran), the director Abrar Alvi explains in detail the making of the 'portrait' (with the movie camera) that testifies to Choti Bahu's reputation as someone whose beauty is perfect and sans any blemish.[6]

The initial filming gave disastrous results with distortions in Meena Kumari's face and the problem was finally identified to be the choice of the telephoto lens (75 mm) on the Mitchell camera that had been used. All shots of her face were thereafter shot on a 40 mm lens. A still photography shoot was also held to identify the most flattering angles of Meena Kumari's face and it was agreed that one side would always be shot for profile and the other for any frame that required the three-fourth angle.[7] Alvi's comments help us understand how central the notion of classical beauty was to the imagination of the film and its tragedy.

Bedazzled thus by this beauty, Bhootnath is puzzled by the casual nature of the conversation—its easy affection and intimacy towards a complete stranger, one who suddenly finds himself in a boudoir. It is this unexpectedness that breaks the distances of appropriate behaviour. After all, he is on the floor, a plate of food is given to him and she keeps remarking on his shyness. It is her repeated indulgent, unexpected fondness for him that cause/allow him to look up at her. The gaze has to be resolutely non-erotic—he should not ideally be there at all, leave alone look at her. She too should not be looking at him, except from a protected position of authority. However, rules have already been broken and Bhootnath is recruited to the private mission of bringing a box of 'Mohini *sindhoor*' (vermillion) for Choti Bahu.

Choti Bahu sits on the bed to retrieve money from beneath her pillow. She talks about the ways of the men of the household—their days are for sleeping and their nights are for play with lovers. This means that the women and the servants of the household also have to stay awake, waiting. 'This is why I called you'—she says and briefly the unsaid, unthinkable possibility (does she want this strange man to satiate her?) is aired. The framing of the desires of the mistress by the wooden posts of the marital bed becomes a repeated trope in the film. Abrar Alvi explains his deliberate placement of the bed in the centre of the film, 'an empty bed, symbolic of her life'.[8] The bed as a metonym for desire is established by two strong frames in quick succession: (a) the first of her seated on the bed, her hands sliding under the pillow (Fig. 4.1) and the more powerful breach that follows, (b) the camera crossing into the marital bed, looking at Bhootnath over her shoulders and through the draping gauze (Fig. 4.2). It is clear that there is a heartfelt sorrow that she wants him to assuage.

Fig. 4.1 *Source NFAI*

Fig. 4.2 *Source NFAI*

The scene ends with Choti Bahu sending Bhootnath away saying '*kal milenge*' (we will meet tomorrow)—the meeting extends to another night. The characters and the viewer are kept in this ongoing loop of desire and expectation. It is a loop that had begun with the initial scene of the film (set in the cinematic present of the early twentieth century) and would end with the concluding scene (again, set in the same time frame). The film exists in this interregnum, a coil of longing and expectation and delay, within the outer-narrative of the present helmed by Bhootnath. It is to this outer-narrative/opening scene of the film to which the analysis will now turn.

The Splice of Memory

The notion of time and memory as literary trope and visual palimpsest is embedded from the opening sequence of the film including its title credits. The first frame of the film is a hardbound, worn book in a spotlight—a large looming table lamp in the left foreground of the frame is a faux source of light that the camera inches past. As the credits appear, the camera begins to track very slowly (almost imperceptively) towards the book. The slow tracking of the image of the novel presages the visual style of much of the film—delicacy, discreetness and intimacy of movement. It is as if the camera is hand-held for there seems to be a slight tremor. The camera reaches close enough to fill the frame with the book—the frame fades to black after the director's name. The next frame is a repeat but now the book is being opened by male hands, a direct homage to the literary: the film is an adaptation of a novel and indeed the film will end with the image of the last page of the book being turned. The viewer is also a reader. And the pages dissolve into a long shot of the ruins of a grand house—the pillars and an old fountain (European-style of four nude women arranged back to back) remain the identifying markers for the transitions of memory that the images have to negotiate.

Let us consider the image of the sprawling mansion and how the visual instantiates simultaneously an individual as well as a collective historical past. These two types of pasts may be seen not as mere reflections of each other but as commingled, nested within, mutually enhancing. In an early image, a meta-establishing shot for all that is lost and lamented, labouring bare-backed human figures (pulling down and digging out the ruins) are seen through an archway that evokes a large keyhole (Fig. 5). The camera starts to track around the crumbling walls to show a broader view of the collective labour of digging out the past. The shouts of the labourers (encouraging each other to apply force) and the objects they are trying to pull down are shown without obstruction in a top angle frame. The upper part of a pillar is seen falling into the foreground of the visual space, evoking a direct image of violent and deliberate destruction of past artifacts. The work is interrupted by the announcement of a break by one of the labourers and the men move towards the wings.

Fig. 5 *Source NFAI*

We are now three minutes into the film and are introduced to the protagonist (Bhootnath) in a frontal mid shot. In contrast to the labourers, he is in a suit, his left leg raised with his boot on a ruined wall, a large rolled paper in his hands. His manner, clothes and mien put him at an unsurpassable distance from the labourers and it is this difference that allows a certain kind of viewer to enter his private world, a set of concerns far from the world of the hard but straightforward labour of the workers. The protagonist rolls up the paper (presumably an architectural/engineering plan) as the labourers file past him for their lunch break. The camera tracks closer, keeping him firmly in the centre of the screen. The mood shifts: He fills the frame but does not dominate it. Rather, there is a vulnerability to his gaze. It is in the direction of the viewer but is of something distant, intangible—this uncertainty is in contrast to the authority of the suit and his social distance from the labourers. A top angle shot of the site offers a protective space to the protagonist. He is a small figure who enters from the right of the screen. The frame is dominated by the image of ruination—strongly silhouetted pillars, a lit centre of rubble and hay. His gait is as uncertain as his gaze and he turns to see that lit centre of rubble before sitting down on the low wall around it. The frame is thus of an absent centre, a distracted, small human figure against large, unkempt ruins. The next shot cuts to him in profile and mid-long shot. He is agitated, turns his head (as if listening to the faintest hint of music), then gets up, begins to walk—he gives the sense of looking for something and the instrumental music becomes audible and rises as he moves. Another top angle shot follows: Bhootnath is a small figure looking into the camera—but what this shot now prioritises is a ruined stairway that is in the foreground of the image, running from the left to the centre of the shot. The music is accompanied by a reverberating distant female voice, forcing him to move. The ethereality and again, the height of the voice forces his ascent up the stairway. Stairways and ascents are repeated in the film, perhaps evoking a movement away from horizontality to a more inegalitarian, heightened state—the everyman can only look with aspiration to those who walk on the second floor of the house. It is only the privilege of house-help (in contrast to labourers in the fields, or drivers of palanquins, cooks, etc.) to be able to inhabit the upper floors where the wives of the landlord class reside. The theme of looking up (and the camera's representation of this imbalance) vis-à-vis Bhootnath and Choti Bahu has already been discussed in the previous section.

To return to the opening scene: Bhootnath advances toward the stairway as if the sound is coming from thereabouts and then turns towards the camera. He moves towards it (as the camera slowly pans right) as though approaching something mysterious and unknown. It feels like the camera is awaiting his ascent, imperceptibly guiding his movement and that after he ascends, it becomes his point of view for looking at the ruins. But the tracking frame is perceptibly slower than the walk we have seen thus far. It seems like the protagonist's tentative disturbed inscape is unfolding in a visual vista—the frame of the ruins seen through a net of overgrown vegetation is intercut with shots of his agitated expression. The elongation of time is accomplished through this splicing of image repetitions and becomes the portal of an overwhelming recollection. To underline this, the camera hovers (not quite co-incident with his point of view) and inches to a deep-set lit arch interlaced with spider webs. This dissociation between his point of view and the camera eye is the gap between the immediate sensory encounter with the space and the gathering invisible and still-unacknowledged affect rising within. It is an exceptional moment—the camera continues deeper into the archway, almost beyond what he can physically move, as if it has a mind and desire of its own to know, to probe and to find out. Far and near leaves keep losing and gaining focus in this autonomous movement of the camera. It is an impossible point of view and signals a desire greater than can be expressed by the limb or eye of the protagonist. We are taken to a dreamy, delicately textured frame of focused and unfocussed shapes—dark leaves, white spider-web. There is a return to silence. Bhootnath stops, the camera cuts to framing his figure through aged iron railings, his gaze beyond the viewer. At this moment, his point of view (of ruined walls) slowly superimposes into what the space looked like in the past—a prosperous well-appointed space. The overlap of the two worlds visually (as superimposition) is sustained for several seconds as the camera eye (standing in for the protagonist) pans to the right and the sounds of human voices (from the past) are heard. The sequence cuts again to his disturbed face and there is now a clear voice of a woman calling someone (is it him?) to come.

As discussed in the section previously, the word 'come' sutures visuals representing different 'introductory moments' in the narrative. He utters his first words—'Choti Bahu'—presumably as recognition of a past and as a way to arrest the tension building up within. And again in anticipation of Bhootnath's first meeting with Choti Bahu, a female voice invites him to come and sit down among the ruins. He moves to sit down—the voice is not clearly locatable. He is clearly exhausted as he picks up a clod of earth and begins to pull at the grass. A voiceover (that belongs to him) remembers the past glory of the house, as the camera moves to a close-up that fills the screen with his face. The story is now organised—his voice explains, 'Years ago, when I came from the village, I saw this house for the first time….' He repeats *kya shaan thi* (such grandeur there was!) as his face dissolves into the shot of the central courtyard (of the past, with its proud white pillars and sculpted nudes intact). The pillars tower over the many bare-backed labourers working under it, carrying various goods into the house on their heads—they are adding to the house instead of demolishing it. There are strains of happy instrumental music—the film has stumbled vertiginously into the past and the grip of that past will not loosen for the next two hours of screen-time.

Thematically, the film will now be framed from the point of view of Bhootnath—both his eye and his sensibility. He is the sensitive, young, educated man for whom the future is to unfold—in contrast, the world of Choti Bahu is the world of the landlord's past that is being argued out of existence by more egalitarian philosophies. Yet, the narrative is not a simple ode to the worldly ascent of the newly empowered classes. Rather, it is about the sense of loss that is located in a past moment of interlaced lifetimes. The film's infusive melancholia requires that this loss not be quite locatable in a time or space or frame but pervade the entirety of the plotline.

The final encounter between Choti Bahu and Bhootnath is fated to be in a carriage. The world has shifted under their feet. By this time, the *haveli* is in clear decline, the husband incapacitated. As a desperate attempt to mitigate his illness Choti Bahu decides to meet a *sadhu* (holy man) reputed to have healing powers. Her journey is made late in the night, with Bhootnath as a chaperone, in a horse-carriage. But her husband's elder brother, the louche patriarch, espies her leaving at night with a man not of the family and of considerably lower social standing—this is a grave indiscretion. Consequences must be plotted—landlords will not be taken for granted even as the signs of their decline are everywhere. The carriage sequence is also the last interaction that Choti Bahu will have with anyone in her lifetime: that it is destined to be with Bhootnath, who has been so loyal to her, is telling. The intimate space of the carriage makes this last encounter all the more compact and explosive. The camera watches them through wooden slats—Bhootnath with eyes averted, Choti Bahu looking out—there is the sound of the clop-clop of horses' hooves and wooden wheels (Fig. 6). They, and their gazes, are already occupying different worlds, different horizons. The shot continues with the camera slowly zooming in to her pain-filled eyes, now seen as though behind bars.

Fig. 6 Source NFAI

The carriage is shown cutting across a dark landscape speckled with distant lights. The next frame shows the inside of the carriage for a conversation that Bhootnath initiates—he asks about the health of her husband. It is the first time they are sitting side by side and there is quietness to the exchange that the close shots that follow retain through the play of shadows. When both are framed in mid shot, he leans to her, his eyes on her even as her gaze flows out into some hidden distance. There is both a new egalitarian intimacy, but also the fact that her gaze is directed elsewhere. Her slow speech mimics the speech of the ill and dying. The only time that the slowness and languor are disrupted is when he tells her that he is married. Before he can reveal any more, the carriage comes to an abrupt halt. They are pulled out into the dark. While assailants beat him, her bangled hand is shown clutching the door of the carriage. A man's hand pulls it away—accompanied to the sound of her screams.

It is significant that all through the film Bhoothath had primarily encountered Choti Bahu as a voice—song, invitation, request, surreptitious conversation and now, finally, a scream. It is sound rather than the visual that had represented his idealisation of her. However, it is the visual (with its concomitant shadows and dissolves) that concretises and shapes their impossible relationship. It is the bangled hand (of the carriage scene) that is later discovered as the skeletal hand exhumed in the digging of the *haveli*. Though it has been suggested that 'in the film's terms, this is punishment for her transgressive behavior',[9] one can equally read it as a scene whereby there is an attempt to give an unnameable love privacy and dignity. Indeed, this privacy is reminiscent of their first meeting in her chamber. Though the site has now shifted—there is the move from a safe haven to an exposed, terrifying world—and though there is a more egalitarian encounter (he is not on the floor and indeed is the more ascendant figure at this point) the affect rhymes with that earlier moment due to the discreetness and reticence of the camera.

In the flashback-time of the film, Bhootnath had been young and earnest. Perhaps it was important that the camera initially find him of virginal mind, to better relay on that *tabula rasa* the unfurling of the narrative: his blankness (the beginning of his education in the real world) is the counterpoint to Choti Bahu, who represents the saturation of a gendered (that is inegalitarian) marital relation. In her own way Choti Bahu is innocent—she thinks for example that the reputed efficacy of the *sindhoor* will cause her husband to desire her. Yet, she also emblematises the inequality and helplessness of her side of the marital relation, an inequality only possible in a closed, hierarchical, deeply controlled 'feudal' world, where there can be no exiting actions of freedom. Indeed, if there is freedom at all, it is in the inwardised form of self-destruction (through alcohol), a freedom that only grows by clawing ever deeper into one's body and limb. On the other hand, the 'education/*bildung*' of Bhootnath is the difficult consumption of this unravelling. Though he grows ever more successful in the world and finds himself in a more modern and companionate marriage, there is equally a deep understanding of the sorrow of the world shaped by his experience of Choti Bahu's tragedy. The bookending scenes have him interpreting the world as essentially full of estrangements between self, other and the milieus that one finds oneself embedded in.

Lighting and Shading Desire

V.K. Murthy talks about one of his preferred techniques for sculpting light and shadows in a scene—the use of cutters. 'Sometimes, I used more cutters than lights. That's why several people would tease me—Murthy-saab, you give such a big light and then cut it all out!'[10] He gives the specific example of the *mujra* (dance of the courtesan)—*Saaqiya aaj mujhe neend nahin aayegi* (Cup-bearer, I will not be able to sleep tonight)—a group dance sequence in a large well-lit hall watched by the landlords of the *haveli*. Unconventionally, only the main dancer is lit and all the other dancers in the background are silhouetted—this is not an easy effect to maintain through several movements of both dancers and the camera, and remains one of the striking visual experiments of the film. In this song by a *tawaaif* (one who has no relevance to the emotional graph of the film) this mode of lighting may not have much significance. However, this attention to light and shade gathers new affective force in a later song.

In a film that has to manage many unsaid desires (physical and emotional wants that remain silent due to social strictures), the songs with their stylised visualisations, plaintive tunes and confessional lyrics become an important site of a different order of imagination. The tragic figure of Choti Bahu is so strong that the parallel love story of Bhootnath and Jaba remains peripheral to the affective arc of the movie. While Jaba and Bhootnath are attracted to each other, there are obstacles to their love. Jaba's afflicted love allows further exploration of the idiom of lighting—whereas Choti Bahu moves from being evenly lit (the classical ideal of perfect beauty) to the more patchily lit moments after she surrenders to alcohol, the lighting of Jaba mixes these registers to better represent a more mercurial temperament—this sometimes occurs within a single shot as will be discussed below. Jaba is the daughter of Bhootnath's employer, and as the employers are members of the Brahmo Samaj, Jaba is educated and does not practice *purdah* (the veiling common to upper castes and classes). She is an outspoken and feisty young woman. The initial days of Bhootnath and Jaba's association are innocent but there is a growing attraction that remains a quiet undercurrent till it emerges in its strongest expression in the song *Meri baat rahi mere man mein* (my thoughts have remained in my mind). Bhootnath has just found out that Jaba (who he has romantic feelings for) is to be married to someone else—the social situation precludes any confession on his part or indeed from the usually outspoken Jaba. Instead, he walks out of the compound after an exchange of telling glances. As Bhootnath leaves in silence, now the rejected suitor, the gates of the house close behind him. Jaba runs out and the camera watches her through the bars of the iron gate, making her emotional confinement only too obvious. The camera has finally created a moment for Jaba to break out the chrysalis of the mere love interest (secondary to the pathos of Choti Bahu) and the lyrics of the song echo the need for fuller recognition of her distress.

In this sequence there is thus another meditation through visuality on a type of unfulfilled love—one perhaps in contradistinction to the Choti Bahu-Bhootnath relation and yet one that has its own pathos. 'My thoughts have remained in my mind; I cannot speak of what I feel in this confusion'—the visual treatment of this first line of the song remains an extraordinary moment in the evolution of the song sequence in Hindi cinema and has very few parallels in its virtuosity. One can understand this better by looking at two frames from the single-shot that covers the first two lines—a slow tracking in of the camera from a mid-shot of Jaba to a close-up as she holds her throat with her hands and moves her lips to the words. The shot begins with an even diffused light (Fig. 7A). As the camera moves closer, the lights start to dim till they fade out completely with only the faintest outline of Jaba visible. It is a claustrophobic blanking out (sustained only by sound), so dark that it cannot be represented by a figure in this book. But soon after, a light falls on Jaba's shoulder and another light slowly fills in the rest of the contours of her face—the camera is now very close and intimate with her. The light has not returned to its previous intensity but it is a highly empathetic visual moment (Fig. 7B). Within a few minutes, we have moved from the bright mid-day sunlit courtyard scene to a theatrical gray-scape that is filled with blurred and moving shadows. It is as though dusk has suddenly settled into her house and heart. This grey lighting is then continued through the song—Jaba forming the contrast to the grey with her dark sari and white border. She walks across the screen lip-synching the song, her palms still clutching throat and lips. Tears shimmer in shadow and light as her gaze remains at some fixed off-camera space. This gaze is introverted—as opposed to a gaze directed at a diegetic space or at the audience. It is her introspective spanning of past, present and future destinies—of all that still remains uncertain for her, of promises and betrayals. Once again the lights start to fade on her and this time it is into a classic cinematic dissolve—to images of fond moments she had shared with Bhootnath in the past. The dissolve lasts a few seconds before returning to the frame of the grey present and to her consciousness of emotional loss.

Fig. 7A *Source NFAI*

Fig. 7B *Source NFAI*

The viewer starts to see a pattern to the visual treatment of this mournful solitude: Each time the musical interlude starts between the stanzas of the song, the lights fade out and the frame dissolves to a memory of a past closeness with her lover. The dissolves are sustained for several seconds and do not lose the contours of the present frame. Thus the images are continuously overlapped and the frame that endures is never the past event alone but a present expressive Jaba. Even when the lights are dimmed, her hair remains backlit. Indeed, several of the mid and close frames of Jaba are lit for soft diffused edges. This mitigates the overall greyness of the backdrop and also preempts the grief expressed in the song from engulfing the cinematic moment that stays self-consciously stylistic in its exploration of ill-fated desire. The slow tempo of the song is outdone by an even slower camera. As the song ends we have truly entered the realm of the night—Jaba is engulfed in dark spaces, walking against the horizontal bars of lit window shutters. She turns into the house to climb up the dimly lit stairs just as the song ends and in the last moment of virtuosic shading, the lights on the stairs dim to pitch black. Now only the lit glass of an arched door is visible and the slowly walking Jaba is swallowed up in the darkness of the song-scape and her own impenetrable, crystalline solitude. Then the lights of the door also turn off and only darkness remains.

In that moment of darkness Jaba's life briefly carries resonances of Choti Bahu's loneliness and frustration. The various forms of shading that the visual accomplishes to disassemble barricaded female desires can be similarly studied in the scene that depicts Bhootnath's second meeting with Choti Bahu—this is when he brings her the box of vermillion that she had asked for. She receives him in her bedroom, the only man apart from her husband and the domestic help to step in to that space. The marital bed gains import and centrality in the visual idiom of the scene. She sits on the bed in speckled light, an evocative glass-encased source of illumination keeping attentive company in the frame, especially as the camera moves closer to her, the last frame of the shot emphasising the shading of her face by her sari.

In this space of privacy, she is able to tell Bhootnath about the emptiness of her marriage, with her husband barely home and the elaborate ruse she has to concoct to get him to visit her. Bhootnath listens wide-eyed, moved by her candour and helplessness and leaves after reassuring her that the vermillion will indeed work its magic. Choti Bahu expresses gratitude and if he has felt anything for her, any attraction or fascination, it is hidden from her and the viewer—his body and face are kept in darkness. She asks him to let her know if he needs any help and tells him not to forget her. The camera stays steady on her face and then the frame again fades to black.

We return to Choti Bahu a scene later. She is in the middle of her *shringar* (personal adornment) and it is the beginning of a song-sequence. The camera gently tilts to a compact frame of her hair as it is being combed, to a close-up of her face as she gazes at a hand mirror, slowly moving it in an arc till it comes between her and the camera. The camera becomes voyeuristic, a mirror behind the mirror, returning the gaze to her ringlet-framed face. Choti Bahu's *shringar* is inseparable from the activities of the women tending to her—one combing and braiding her hair to the rhythm of the song, the other towelling her feet. Choti Bahu fills the screen with eyes, brow, smile, profile and locks of hair. Her elaborate dressing up—*sindhoor,* kohl, gold earrings and necklace—is contrasted to the single-drape saris of the unadorned servant women.

The song ends as it had begun—with the mirror. But instead of the private confined space of the hand mirror, we have the large dressing table mirror now reflecting her husband. The anticipation (on what will follow next in their marital relationship) hinges on the efficacy of the *sindhoor*. She begs her husband to look fully at her at least once. He reluctantly obliges—in contradistinction to his reluctant gaze, the camera rushes in. An initial formal portraiture frame (Fig. 8) turns into an extreme close-up (one of the eyes, *bindi* and the pearls of her forehead jewellery)—this is a transgressive violation of the formal portraiture tradition and a shot that insists on a more visceral intimacy. This image mirrors and extends

Bhootnath's first glimpse of her (see Fig. 3)—the posed, idealised vision of beauty.

Fig. 8 *Source NFAI*

The thrusts and forays of the camera is a recurring motif of the film. There is a productive tension between the limited visual access of characters (including their psychological and social limitations) and the willingness and desire of the camera to move into those forbidden spaces, to gaze, appreciate and probe. The camera remains invested in a continual and open admiration of Choti Bahu, even as a tension is productively created by this contrast of the admiring camera and varied kinds of indifference and blindness (the husband) or the suppressed, respectful gaze of the hierarchically lower-class male (Bhootnath). Choti Bahu is framed by these three gazes (two human males and one camera)—and care is taken that Bhootnath's and the husband's gaze do not directly interact.

To return to the scene that demanded visceral intimacy: Choti Bahu's husband lets her know why she can never offer him all that he needs—for example, he asks 'Can you dance for me? Can you share my alcohol?' It is a shattering moment, to be asked for the unthinkable, that which will overturn all the moral codes that she was raised with in her upper-caste family. But it is thus also the last frontier to brave to stake a claim for legitimate marital passion. Alvi takes credit for a new archetype of sexuality in this scene: instead of beseeching at her husband's feet, the wife is at eye level, moving ever closer to him (Fig. 9). He considers this 'a signature scene' that marked the film as his—the signature effect he refers to is that of the 'trolley [moving] toward her and continues as she starts approaching the trolley'.[11] For Alvi, this shot highlighted both the egalitarian sexuality as well as the shock invested in that moment. It was something that even his contemporaries such as Murthy recognised as new and striking. Alvi claims this as proof that the film was not ghost-directed by Guru Dutt—a rumor that had plagued Alvi's career.[12] It is worth noting that Alvi did not direct a second film and so it is a charge that weighs on him, for *Sahib Bibi aur Ghulam* is commonly accepted as a classic. That Abrar chooses one particular shot execution as proof of his auteurship underlines the thesis of this chapter—the identity of black and white films of this era, especially those produced under the Guru Dutt banner, had been strongly invested in a unique visual signature of storytelling, where the visual code was given as much importance as the explicit thematics involved.

Fig. 9 *Source NFAI*

After hearing her husband speak thus, Choti Bahu has to find a way to get the alcohol and decides to turn again to her trusted '*ghulam*' Bhootnath. This is his third meeting with her and it is to be even more shrouded in secrecy and shame. The shame is so great that he comes to her through a secret passage and doorway. The request for alcohol is stated under the cover of darkness and the security of the bulky poster-bed serves to shield her from the gaze of the camera. At the start of the scene, the point of view is Bhootnath's. He enters Choti Bahu's bedroom and looks around: he has traversed a far distance (socially and psychologically) from the time he had been only looking at the floor in the first meeting. In this third meeting, the camera pans from an open doorway to a bed that is covered in patches of dark. The figure of Choti Bahu is barely visible—shame is darkness. The camera has to track in closer to locate her (even as she asks Bhootnath to approach). By the next frame, Bhootnath has walked closer to the bed, his face half-revealed in the light from the doorway—again, shame and darkness veil both of them. The camera looks over his blurred contours to her standing with her back to both Bhoothnath and the camera. She is facing an ominously lit window. 'It is better if you don't see me today,' she tells him, for such is the weight of her secret. He wonders what it might be, coming closer and she says that she has only him to trust. At the moment that Choti Bahu decides to tell him what she wants the camera bypasses both Bhoothnath and the bed and tracks very close to the back of her head, a sliver of profile and hair lit by the window (Fig. 10). 'Bring me alcohol', she says. The music peaks in distress and the camera breaks the stillness of the visual treatment of the scene by rushing to capture Bhootnath's distress. His face is a dark grotesque mask with patchy smears of light. Choti Bahu's close-up is the answer to his anxiety—she is in a calm profile, her *sindhoor* prominent. A gentle light on the face sculpts her resolve. Choti Bahu moves to the light of the window—even though she is unashamed, she does not want his full direct gaze and keeps her back to him. They continue to speak.

He moves towards her, his moral solicitousness perhaps an unwarranted intimacy—in this mood, he forces a confrontation and she eventually looks directly at him (Fig. 11).

Fig. 10 *Source NFAI*

Fig. 11 *Source NFAI*

Bhootnath refuses to obey her this time (perhaps this is a moment of premonition for she will indeed come to ruin from addiction) and walks away, stopped only by her asking him 'You like me very much, don't you?' This last is a frame where his back to her and her body in the direction of the camera brings to the fore an uncertain, surreptitious desire, one that had run like a vein through the filmic text but had never been expressed directly either in speech or posture. Bhootnath was unusually positioned in the hierarchy—though he lived among domestic servants, he was not of their class in demeanour, caste or education. This uncertainty of position always radiated an extra element of forbidden desire—whereas earlier Choti Bahu was clearly positioned in a more maternalist/kinship role (he had given her *sindhoor*), now the shift in object of what she was asking for (alcohol and moreover alcohol as aphrodisiac, a repeated motif of the patron-*tawaif* world) brings a new, if fleeting, inter-subjective tension. This newness is suggested by the positioning of their bodies in the space of her bedroom, her bed looming large, the closed though lit windows, her looking up, their faces close together, lit as if they were, or could be, lovers.

The entry of alcohol into the triangulated dynamics between the aristocratic husband, the desperate wife and the obliging admirer is bound to overturn carefully rehearsed social roles. When Bhootnath later comes to Choti Bahu's chambers to leave some money in her safekeeping, her formal distance and demeanour are not present any longer. Instead, she is supine on the bed, on her stomach, her bare legs folded in the air in a carelessness that we have never seen before. Her unkempt hair and slurry speech indicate inebriation. As she twists and turns in the bed, asking for more alcohol, he is asked to come closer—she pushes the end of her sari at him, where the keys to the safe are knotted and asks him to unknot the keys. What might have been a commonplace action is eroticised—his touching her sari, the unknotting, his presence so close to her bed and face. The visual treatment of the scene is to stay with a dimness that grants them enough privacy even as the viewer is now effectively a voyeur. The camera is non-judgemental to Choti Bahu; each frame of her is at the level of her bed, not looking down or up but within the ambit of her point of view. It is only when Bhootnath tells her that she is addicted to alcohol that the camera moves behind his shoulder and looks down at her. Yet he cannot leave and she too wishes to keep talking, to keep him there in the room with her notwithstanding all the shame. She says she drinks because her husband wants her to and also because she is unhappy. Even as she writhes in bed, he bends, more delicately solicitous. But the moment of non-verbal intimacy does not last and she is back in the position of supplicant. She denies addiction and speaks instead of seeking her husband's love—the camera once again empathetically frames her as an equal by moving to her eye-level. Bhootnath does not relent—he tells her she should be ashamed (*sharam* is the Arabic origin-word for both Hindi *sharam*, and the Indo-European/English shame). In response to such preaching, Choti Bahu turns defiant. Staggering to her feet, she throws the glass to the floor to say how proud she is of her husband being the first man of that landed family to stay home and be faithful to his wife. Her head sways as she speaks, the camera swaying with her, keeping her in its view, still sympathetic. When he grabs the bottle from her and holds her wrist, she is horrified and the camera totters forward echoing her indignation, moving very close to her face. As she screams at him to leave the room the camera also moves back respectfully as if obeying her. Bhootnath is transfixed in shock—the camera tracks around the marital bed as she collapses on it and Bhootnath leaves the room. The tragedy can only spiral out of hand henceforth.

Few sequences represent the culmination of that tragedy than the visualisation of the song *Na jao saiyan* (Don't go beloved)—the song demonstrates a simultaneous display of seduction and grief. This inseparability of seduction and grief is the clue to the film's imagination of the foredoomed and the tragic. The scene starts with the camera looking at the couple (Choti Bahu and her husband) through the frame of the bed in which Choti Bahu is lying down. There is already defeat and pleading in her voice, an open desperation that tries to smile and keep faith. The seduction is in the same register as madness in the stereotypical tropes employed—distortions of face and hair. Choti Bahu's breaking into song is clearly a surprise for her husband. The camera continues to linger on Choti Bahu's features and limbs in tightly composed frames but the energy of the song comes from the precise rhythms of editing—each shot is timed and cut perfectly to the line of the lyric. Her facial expressions too synch to this pacing. The husband watches with an impassive face as she beckons him with eyes and voice. The camera plays the mediator, the marital bed remaining an important element of the composition. Indeed the song never leaves the bed. The camera tracks at the level of her moving body, watching her through the gaps in the carvings on the bed. It rises from the level of the bed only when the couple rises. But the elevated position does not sustain itself, for, at the end of the song, the drunk Choti Bahu collapses on the floor. Her husband walks away in disgust. The camera takes her point of view as he tells her that it is the duty of the wife to live and die in her husband's house—the outside world is for men alone. She begs for release and asks to be taken to where the courtesans live so that she can be a part of his world. He tells her to not have such absurd ideas: she should behave and live like the other daughters-in-law of the house. The scene ends with his exit and her weeping in the dark doorway of a room framed by curtains and tassels. It is a repeated frame—the same as the one where she had thanked Bhootnath for the *sindhoor*. In the past, it had been a site of hope and optimism. Now it is a site of a visual collapse: the camera does not shift to her level but tilts down. Her head is towards the lower edge of the frame and her feet stretch into the upper line, a visual distortion that underlines her evisceration, the final overturning of the classical portrait that had been so closely associated with her in the film (Fig. Zero, the only image in the book accessed from public sources. See page 210).

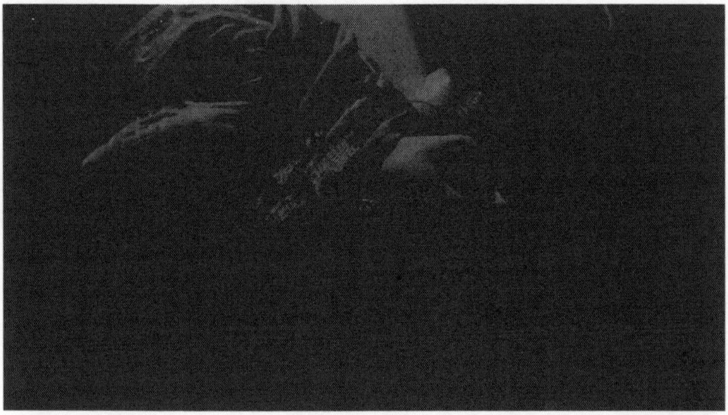

Fig. Zero Source NFAI

After this scene—one which literalises an overturning of all hope—the rest of the film confirms a steady decline. This decline culminates in the assault on Choti Bahu as she travels with Bhootnath to see a healer for her incapacitated husband—the scene has been discussed. Since we are cued to her fate primarily through Bhootnath, we discover via the domestic help Bansi that her husband dies soon after her disappearance and that the family fortunes have also been destroyed. She serves as a metonym for a whole landed world that could not cope. In the last scene of the film, Choti Bahu's grave is abruptly discovered—it is clear that her elder brother-in-law had her murdered for her indiscretion with Bhootnath and had her buried within the *haveli* itself. The discovery of the body is treated not just as a plot-reveal but is shot in a manner that captures the mood of waiting that this film has so consistently achieved through the measured, controlled camera movements and the use of long dissolves and superimposition. As the labourers uncover from the earth a skeletal hand, the camera takes Bhootnath's point of view, slowly panning over the earth even as his imagination superimposes a smiling Choti Bahu in her prime (the portraiture mode again in full finery) against the ribcage of her actual skeleton (Fig. 12). This film has taken a distinctive approach in its extended use of superimpositions—while sometimes the superimpositions indicate the passing of time, at other times they are used to bind disparate narratives and images that have a common affective core—for example, the key affects of waiting or decay.

Fig. 12 *Source NFAI*

With the final superimposition—the portrait over the skeleton—the film achieves a tentative closure. There is no more waiting. Bhootnath realises what has happened and walks away to a waiting carriage with Jabba outside the *haveli*. In contrast to the high tragedy of Choti Bahu (and Bhootnath's memories of her), Jabba's waiting is more quietly hopeful, more anchored. There are different kinds of waiting: it cannot be located in any one person's aspiration in this film. Rather, it is embedded in the languorous sensuous visual treatment of troubled desires, unattainable joys and the many ways in which people wait for deliverance and strive to make peace.

Conclusion: Fade to Colour

This book has sought to understand the aesthetics of black and white on its own terms—neither as lack nor as existing purely in the 'shadow' cast by its future (the advent of colour). Rather, black and white as the evocative range of shadow and greyscale, as the framing and pacing of action all existed within a fully fleshed visual aesthetic that was agnostic towards whatever was explicitly thematised as 'plot'. Even in this book it has been a certain kind of heartbreaking labour to cut the number of images—there is the logistics of printing and pricing, of quality to quantity but further, there is also the conceptual deception involved in reducing movement to stillness. Nevertheless, we have taken heart from the fact that restoring filmic movement to stills is also perhaps a restoration towards an older tradition of photographs and accompanying text. For what the black and white film shares with the photographic tradition is the manipulation and play of shadow—its elongations, doublings and dominations. The shadow in the cinema discussed in this book had achieved a stature and autonomy—of contrast and monumentality, of the menace of the city or the spectrality of haunted space and architecture. The studio allowed a level of control and freedom and atmospherics that the outdoors (especially in colour) could not. Whatever the achievements of that latter world—preeminently in colour and the outdoors—it does not take away from that historical niche where a different aesthetics was in sovereign play. Indeed, as has been noted by many scholars and practitioners, it took a long time for a developed aesthetic of colour to emerge. For example, as scholar Nasreen Munni Kabir discussed with actor Waheeda Rehman, colour film did not have sophisticated lighting through the 1970s and 1980s; 'every inch of the set was lit with the same intensity. No shading, no pools of darkness to create atmosphere.'[1]

Waheeda Rehman agrees, adding that in 'the early days they wanted to show as many colours as possible—everything had to be bold and brash. Indeed to show they were making a film in colour rather than making the story work.'[2] Rachel Dwyer who examines the visual culture of the *mise en scène* in Hindi cinema writes of the shift that colour wrought 'from texture and light contrast, to the use of colour coordination and filters as major features'.[3] As reputed cinematographer and director Govind Nihalani also comments, unlike black and white films where cinematographers depended on lighting to provide tonal separations and sense of depth, colour was able to do the same with different hues 'even if the lighting in a frame is comparatively flat'.[4] This change in approach to contrast or tonalities also extended to the increasing preference for shooting outdoors—'the use of landscape as spectacle'[5]—and away from the controlled lighting of studio spaces.

It is worth contemplating what the studio space in particular offered to black and white cinema: several experimentations of shadows in composition. The control of sharp sources of illumination (and equally the cutting out and sculpting of light as discussed in V.K. Murthy's cinematography earlier) became less likely when the scenes began to move from the studio to the outdoors. Several films from the late 1940s onwards experimented with certain scenes being shot in the outdoors, such as Raj Kapoor's *Barsaat* (Rain, 1949) and Bimal Roy's *Do Bigha Zamin* (Two Bighas of Land, 1953). As colour became the norm, so did the shooting of outdoor scenes, leading to an invariable shift in visual aesthetics. The case of *Taxi Driver* directed by Chetan Anand and starring his brother Dev Anand (as the taxi driver) offers some insights into this context. Released in 1954, the film tells the story of a taxi driver in the city of Bombay—the film has long sequences shot outdoors. Not only do the film's opening credits show a dapper cigarette smoking taxi driver plying his clients across the city, even the credits playfully include the 'City of Bombay' under its list of 'Guest Artists'. In this moment of written acknowledgement one gets the sense of outdoor visuality as the dominant note of this black and white film (in noticeable contrast to the aesthetic of the studio lighting). Working with largely natural light conditions, mostly a harsh overhead sun that makes for sharp shadows, the film depends on movement—both of the taxi and the cityscape—to craft its telling. 'Location shooting in the city is extended into a textural principle of the image and a sequencing principle between images.'[6] There is admirable ease in its navigation of the outdoors. Yet one can see the tension: for, eight minutes into the film, one has the first dramatic situation of the film—two thugs trying to take advantage of a young woman. At this moment of tension what the viewer realises is that the dramatisation can still only take place within the studio—for one sees the taxi glide into a studio space. The emotional tenor of the scene requires the sharp 'night lighting' (purportedly the headlights of the taxi and some ambient light) of the studio—this demonstrates the dependence that these films had on shadows for creating mood with greyscale. Though the city can provide a dynamic backdrop it cannot yet serve as a site for the sustained and affective unfolding of the visual.

The diverse flowering of both greys and the accompanying shadows have been studied in this book and one would like to suggest that this mode of reading would also give a broader insight into some stylistic devices that travelled between various productions of the time period. The effort here is to distil what was discussed regarding specific films, as well as evoke some of the stronger moments of the films of the era that were not discussed—this is to make the point of the larger, shared and inherited aesthetic that pervaded the historical moment. For example, *Mahal* with its story of haunted and haunting love extends the *noir* genre in revealing ways. The architectural elements of the setting (clock towers, domes and sprawling grounds) are lit up in with dramatic accents, various shades of dark and light permeate the affective exchanges between space and its spectrality. In the same year that *Mahal* was released, another film Mehboob Khan's *Andaz*

(Style, 1949) made its mark as the highest grossing Indian film of the time. Ravi Vasudevan has argued that *Andaz*'s 'narrative strategy and the elements of its publicity campaign were oriented to generate an image of modernity for the Indian audience'.[7] It is important to remember that cosmopolitan modernity here was not just in terms of theme (a fashionable young woman's dalliance with two men) but in terms of visual aesthetic—what is evoked is the Hollywood world of glamour photography, 'smooth, silken surfaces' with its variable diffusers, all especially important to light the heavily-made up female actor's face without the make-up showing in the intensely bright lights.[8] The first scene that has the dynamic of the romantic triangle has the man who is courting her playing on the piano (she thinks of him as a friend) while she and her lover lean on the piano listening to him. All the visual components of the scene (the piano, the clothing and the backdrop) are lit to show high social standing—instead of the strife we expect from this 'love triangle', we have instead a dissonant, ironic harmonisation. The camera looks over the shoulders of the lovers (played by Raj Kapoor and Nargis) but frames the 'outsider' to the love (played by Dilip Kumar) at the centre of the frame. The effect of this triangular visual evocation is more serene than conflictual. There is a reining in of any subtext of shadows (the shadows are entirely incidental to the source of light)—an evenly lit canvas is the hallmark of the film. This distinct visual style (the lighting of easeful wealth that overrides characters' psychic traumas) was to prove influential for many films over the coming decades.

An opposition to this style of *Andaz* is evident in the contemporaneous *Aag*—in *Aag* there is the use of strong contrasts of lighting. Here shadow is used as a tool of menace, one that speaks out beyond light and dark into a richer ambiguity and anxiety of expression. *Aag* begins with the fire of the title—fire can both sanctify peaceful matrimony and domestic religion, on the one hand, as well as evoke the pain of burning skin. This is what happens as the plot progresses: fire burns both the professional space (the proscenium theatre) and the body of the protagonist—half of his face turns into singed creases that appear more grotesque due to the stark lighting. The idea of evocative and jagged contrast is extended from the individual artist to the nameless urban intruder in Raj Kapoor's production of *Jagte Raho* (Stay Alert, 1956). This film was a satire that was bold and experimental in its adoption of darkness as a dominant visual backdrop—the entire film takes place in the course of a single night. As the thirsty peasant (who has come to the city in search of employment) wanders from apartment to apartment in search of drinking water, he has hardly any words to utter—he is the (mostly) silent witness to all the hypocrisies he witnesses in different homes of the housing colony. In the first scene of the film, as all the policemen of the city (some sprightly, some sleepy) call out to each other to be alert, the backdrop is the deep night of empty city roads. One can see how the shadows help giganticise the city. Whereas in *Aag* giganticism is the relation of the artist's body to proscenium space, in *Jagte Raho*, this is unimaginably scaled to the vulnerable (rural, thus intrinsically out of place) human body vis-à-vis the monumentality of the city. Whereas shadows in *Aag* helped link the human to the artistic, in *Jagte Raho*, the human is now scaled downward to an infinitesimal point in relation to the social—the social as embodied in the shadows of the metropole, vast and overflowing the frames. Further, the giganticism is not just neutral but actively hostile—the smaller and more vulnerable the figure, the more he is persecuted (the film ends with the city turning against him, calling him a thief, seeking to beat and arrest him). Towards the end of the film, there is a wide shot of the building façade with several storeys of lit windows and door, filled with angry, gesticulating masses—their wrath is turned towards the minuscule, stranded peasant-figure. The shot is a somber exploration of the grays of the night as they turn against the atomised human—the absence of light is here the absence of kindness or the humbler light of recognition.

A similar predatory moral code is evident even in films that take on benevolent moralism such as *Do Ankhen Barah Haath* (Two Eyes

Twelve Hands, 1957). This film is about a progressive jailor's attempt to reform prisoners. Lighting is the key to a film with such binaristic notions of good and evil. This is demonstrated in the shift of the visual-scape from prison to the barren outdoors where the good warden takes his prisoners, seeking to inculcate in them the value of hard work. The task of their labour is to transform aridity into fertility. In a critical scene in the film, the six men ponder running away—all that holds them back is the image of a pair of eyes (the warden's). The entire face is in darkness except for a slit bar of light that falls only on the eyes. The gaze re-imprisons them—where the dark bars of the impersonal jail could not hold them in, the lit, disembodied gaze of trusting love, of the silent coercive call of conscience, invites them back into the fold.

The film-maker Bimal Roy, discussed at length in this book, works with a similarly clarified moral world. Whatever the explicit plot mechanisms—be it *Do Bigha Zamin* (Two Measures of Land, 1953) with its tragic story of labour, or *Devdas* (1955) with its heartbroken alcoholic protagonist or *Madhumati* (1958) with its outdoor canvas of love and nature—the cinema of Roy explores, equally, an intricately realised emotional spectrum. His control of visual language maps intuitively at every step with the protagonists's inner world—this is through his mastery of editing and pacing and the use of unembellished imagery (such as prison bars, stairways, boats and rivers) that immediately take on allegorical quality. Towards the end of *Devdas*, the viewer finds the protagonist confined to a train—it is both confinement as well as freedom, as he simply moves nomadically from station to station without a sense of where he is going or what he is fleeing from. There is a movement, in just a few shots, from a self-assured traveller to an image of complete alcoholic collapse. This is accomplished through Roy's use of the contrast between the confinement of the carriage (as a stable internal space) and its swift and abrupt transformation into the chaos of the outside (through the images of the burning coal of the train, its heavy, thick winding black smoke, the jagged noise of the pistons and wheels, the lone and strong headlights of the hurtling train against the vast black of the Indian countryside at night). This ability to integrate the actor's performance into an articulation of shadows continues in *Sujata* and *Bandini*. Actors move in spaces delineated by patterns of shadow that mirror a half-lit psyche—it is this charting that makes Roy's films seem so perceptive and seamless. Be it a sense of entrapment or anguish or serenity, there is a perfect continuity between face and light, pace and action.

In both of Guru Dutt's films studied in this book, *Pyaasa* and *Kaagaz ke Phool*, the artist stands in the shadows of persecution, a misunderstood shadow that indicts society's myopia and apathy. Through the auditorium scenes in *Pyaasa* (with the poet standing in light at the far end of the hall while all the people are shapes in shadow) the narrative draws our attention to the willing blindness of the audience, their collectivist thinking blended with the darkness in which they stand. This is a new form of critique, a lyric resistance that is backed by cinematography that often tries to push the film into as low light conditions as possible—this is technically achieved through Murthy's gambits in film exposure. *Kaagaz ke Phool* is a rare romance where the characters rarely talk/perform love—the longings between the married studio director and the actress are doomed to a gulf of silence that can only be accessed by the camera. The expression of love is done by the light and dark planes of the film studio, the camera moving between and around them, sometimes as a great exhalation, for it is the only accomplice they have—their love that can only live in studio shadows. In fact, the shadows have to act on their behalf. The theme of the unbridgeability between artist and patron, man and woman, private (art) and public (ridicule) can only be resolved in both *Pyaasa* and *Kaagaz ke Phool* by an individual's denunciation of society—either by walking into the horizon or by submitting to anonymous oblivion and death.

A final, brief reference can be made to a contemporary film that stood at the other end of the spectrum in terms of its visual and public opulence: K. Asif's *Mughal-e-Azam* (The Great Mughal, 1960). Shot on a lavish scale and budget, the film had only three reels in colour. Popular with several generations of film lovers, it was colourised and re-released (2004) with digitally mastered sound and makes for an interesting study on the 'aspiration' of colour from the 1960s. It has been asked whether chemical changes in an existing art object (like adding colour to black and white film) would change 'its authentic aesthetic value'.[9] Asking this question also requires keeping in mind that the songs that K. Asif shot and released in colour already assume that colour had become the very 'template of splendor'.[10] In contrast to this view of colour as splendour that has now become critical and commercial commonsense, this book imagines another fully realised aesthetic of splendour. What is significant in the distinction between the aesthetics of *Mughal-e-Azam* and *Sahib Bibi aur Ghulam* is less colour but rather the relation of colour to an agential camera. In *Mughal-e-Azam*, the nature of the endless grandeur of the court forces the camera to travel in documentary fashion, moving from one ossified spectacle to another. In contrast, the camera in *Sahib Bibi aur Ghulam* (and other films discussed in the book) is unburdened by colour and its attendant spectacularisations—rather, black and white cinema celebrates a camera that has almost achieved autonomy from the expressed or stifled desires of characters or plot points. Such a camera has true freedom, moving respectfully and attentively into secret spaces and can be playful, intimate, inviting, lingering, transgressive and melancholic by turns and within the same breath. It innovates in the image, in its ardency of light and shade—it is private, unhurried, expressive, a navigation of serendipities—and reveals a final, last outspreading of the desire and beauty of an era.

Outro: Reel Number 13

The decision to write this book emerged from our artistic and academic trajectories intersecting over the question of how to develop a vocabulary to speak about the visual aesthetics of a cinema that had left an indelible imprint on the infancy of the nation. The same aesthetics made its presence felt in the terrain of our childhoods in the 1980s when these movies and film-makers continued to be celebrated in popular culture via reruns on television and cassettes played on VHS (Video Home Systems). Kamal Amrohi, Madhubala, Meena Kumari, Ashok Kumar, Raj Kapoor, Bimal Roy, Guru Dutt, Nargis, Nutan and Abrar Alvi, came to represent a wistfully exhumed cinematic footprint. More recently, the iconic black-white-grey images from that time, stark to our colour-biased internet-weary eyes, reminded us that perhaps we had not given sufficient thought to what those assertive visual articulations represented to a collective consciousness that had shaped several decades of artists and viewers in India. The irony of this preoccupation with visual form, at a time when our engagement with the format was as far removed as possible from the original format of the cinema (35 mm), was not lost on us.

Even though neither of us was born at the time of the films' first theatrical release, our viewings were from television telecasts and cassettes played at home—for me it was the highlight of summer vacations in Mangalore (with gratitude to that archaic institution called the video rental library) and for Nikhil Govind these were viewings during school years in Burma (he wonders if the films were smuggled/pirated). Some of the films came to us via the weekly screenings of classics on the national television channel Doordarshan. When we first began to watch these films together, some six years ago, it was concerning the question of the earliest influences on our visual and storytelling sensibilities (Guru Dutt, I said without hesitation) and the format of our shared encounters were compact discs viewed through DVD players. Our digital consumption of the films was reinforced but in a completely new idiom during more recent viewings, often on YouTube or Netflix or Amazon Prime. However, not only were our viewings on different formats reifying the evolution of cinema but they were also bringing to the fore new enabling such as watching the same shot again and again, often down to fractions of a second. Often we viewed films with muted sound and without subtitles so that the images and performances could speak louder to us. This diminution of the screen from the grand theatres of the 1940s to the 1960s (when these movies were released) to the multitude of digital copies whose formats mechanically adjusted to the dimensions of the television or computer screens, has been to us an invitation to see the films not entirely stuck in a historical space or mood but as ongoing encounters.

Both of us grew up in families that celebrated vintage Hindi films and our parents sang to us popular melodies from these films: this is to share that the affinity for the craft was more intuitive than academic for much of our lives. I studied Mass Communication (at the AJK Mass Communication Research Centre, Jamia Millia Islamia, New Delhi) in the mid-1990s and worked as an independent professional in the media industry for a decade. My early assignments were as Assistant Director in film projects, where one of the main duties was to keep a record of the filming, especially the continuity (of action, props, costume and so on). Watching cinema as one frame after another—each filled with details to track continuity—served as dependable training and foundation for this project and indeed for my 'other life' as a novelist. It was an extraordinary privilege to have studied the craft prior to one's first acquaintance with a computer and before everything turned digital: the experience (anxiety and thrill) of slipping hands inside a changing bag to load 16 mm film in its magazine entirely by touch, to feel the weight and vibration of the Arriflex BL camera against bone, to light a space and calculate exposure on film, to hold one's breath in a darkened room as the film (returned from the laboratory) is screened for the first time, to watch sprockets squeak on a Steenbeck editing machine, to cut and splice celluloid to tell a story—film became a tangible object and moving aesthetic at the same time.

This is not to romanticise film or film-making, for my life as a practitioner taught me early enough that I was temperamentally ill-suited to the industry and the dynamics between distance and belonging has marked my knotty relationship with the craft. Nonetheless, it took Nikhil Govind's repeated insistence that a scholar who has laboured on a film set was not a common occurrence that initiated this project. While we worked together at every stage, we agreed that I would compose the voice and structure of the manuscript and this advertently led to a crucial reconnection with a life-trajectory that had trailed away.

As my career took me from film sets to television studios to classrooms to book-writing, and as digital images became the norm, I never expected to work with or touch film again. But it was not till the early weeks of 2020, when I went to the National Film Archive of India (NFAI) in Pune to collect images for this publication that I found myself looking at the familiar curl of celluloid again. A time-lapse of 24 years—so much had changed and so much had remained the same. The redbrick edifice of the NFAI evoked the intense familiarity of all government education/research establishments that one has plodded through as a scholar and citizen. There is that unassailable sensation of entering a time warp: space where a day will almost always unfurl at an unhurried pace. It is a realm that begs a special reserve of patience from researchers—the work as much in negotiating the bureaucratic apparatus as in the archival material one seeks to study.

My journey in this space started with the Documentation Department that has a database of images (production stills or screen grabs) from various films. There being no clear pattern to the nature or quantities of images available for each film, it became obvious soon enough that this database cannot provide the specific frames that are referenced in our manuscript. I was then directed to the Film Preservation Department where a kindly and resourceful official confirmed that of the nine films on my list, four had been digitised and five were still celluloid in cans that would have to be removed and transported from the NFAI vault which is located elsewhere in the same city. The digitised films were *Sujata*, *Bandini*, *Pyaasa* and *Kaagaz ke Phool*. The quality of the screen grabs from these digitised copies did not do justice to the visual finesse of these films but working with digital versions was a constraint of the project that we had already accepted. In the meanwhile, I was told that the other five films—*Aag*, *Mahal*, *Barsaat*, *Seema* and *Sahib Bibi aur Ghulam*—would come from the vault. A day later, all but the last title had arrived in green circular cans stacked one atop another, lining the tungsten-lit corridor of the department where I stood wonderstruck that all the films I had watched since childhood were in front of me—the casual carelessness of their stacking, in a narrow passageway of old equipment and metal shelves where staff scurried all day, was at odds with how privileged I felt. Nonetheless, there they were, the films we had written about, roughly between 12 to 16 spools for each film. The quantity of footage in each can varied but mostly contained about 10–15 minutes of screen time. The films, however, were still not directly accessible to me. I had to wait for a technician to spool it on the Steenbeck machine and run it till we found the specific image that he would mark with a piece of white tape and set aside in a new stack. It was not clear how the marked frames would be turned into digital images for the book but we kept at the process, reel after reel, in the hope of permissions and guidelines trickling down through a hierarchy of officialdom. Just one more day in a capricious archive, one more night in a cold hotel room and gnawing anxiety as the week progressed, especially about not yet sighting the cans of *Sahib Bibi aur Ghulam* in the corridor stacks. Where is it? I kept asking the kindly official. Missing, she said.

Sahib Bibi aur Ghulam, released in 1962, the only directorial offering from Abrar Alvi, the last film produced by Guru Dutt in visual partnership with V.K. Murthy, often rated among the finest performances in Meena Kumari's oeuvre, is an extraordinary film not only in its craftsmanship but for the unfailing adulation it has enjoyed from film enthusiasts since its release. The film with its overwrought melodrama and patchy plotting is not without flaws but in the writing of this project, we remained in agreement that this film represented the summation of the black and white aesthetics of its generation. There simply isn't another film quite like it.

'The master is not in location,' the official told me (and by this, she meant the master copy of the film that was in the archive's safekeeping was not in its designated slot in the vault), 'and the other copy is missing four reels'. Missing? How can that be? The blood had seeped from my face and my sorrow was not entirely comprehensible to the other person. 'It is only misplaced and will turn up, nothing to worry'. Her kindness and reassurance only wrung my heart. 'This is not about my book,' I tried to explain, 'really it is not, but to lose anything of this film is to lose a national treasure.' There may be other copies of the film free-floating in the universe but the copies at NFAI belonged to the nation, kept at the trust of a tax-paying, trusting public. I understood the inevitability of loss but not of apathy and struggled to contain the heartache, a sense of bleakness about my work. How removed we are as scholars, I thought, from this other world of numbering and preserving; we were talking of aesthetics in abstraction when the films were languishing somewhere or disappearing.

Someone tried to assuage my distress by suggesting that the film was on YouTube. Yes, I know, I said, but it is not the same.

Not the same—this thought never left me when I watched the reels run at the archive. One of the challenges of writing this book was presenting still images to the reader while talking of the sensibility of motion. Something was happening in reverse to me in the archive—

for the first time since we began this project, I felt the deepest pleasure in the immaculate stillness of the image and then childlike delight at watching that image become motion when run (24 frames in a second) through the machine. No less wondrous are the patterns running alongside one edge of the strip that turn into sound. The other chastisement of the celluloid was how easily I had overlooked the squarish dimension of 35 mm film—our eyes and sensibilities had become so accustomed to the stretched rectangular orientations of contemporary cinema that when discussing a composition, we had not accounted for the entire frame, just the part of the frame that had been adapted to the widescreen ratio. In other words, for the first time since we started this project, I was able to see the totality of the cinematographer's composition, especially the top and bottom edge of the frame and it was a rediscovery that I will always cherish. It also brought a pang of regret that so much of our analysis of composition had been of an altered viewing (purely in terms of what we saw in that frame) and for authors of a book on visual aesthetics that is not an easy thought to live with. Watching the 35 mm film, I found that the eye travelled on the image differently and one reveled in the elegance of the 4:3 dimension (rather than the more prevalent widescreen ratio of 2.35:1). And perhaps I never felt that gratification more than when I finally got to watch the reels of *Sahib Bibi aur Ghulam* on the boxy monitor of the Steenbeck.

The four missing cans arrived the following day, though can number 13 was lined with fungus and had to be left alone. The only image in this book that has not come from NFAI was inside this can—we have sourced that image from the internet and marked it as Fig. Zero (see page 195) to register our concern about the larger question of the fate of ageing film. It is possible that this affected reel of the film will be cleaned and treated, just as perhaps the master copy of the film will be found and restored to its location in the vault (I did not dare ask of its fate) but it does not address a more fundamental question, that of institutional responsibilities.

It was my fourth day in the archive. All the images on my list had been identified and marked on the reels and now we needed to find a way to get a digital copy. It had been done before in one specific manner. In the early 1980s, Arun Khopkar began work on his study of Guru Dutt's films: *Guru Dutt: Teen Anki Shokantika* was published in Marathi in 1985 and was translated to English by Shanta Gokhale as *Guru Dutt: A Tragedy in Three Acts* in 2012. Khopkar claims his to be one of the first books to print images that came from 'frames of the film in motion rather than publicity stills'.[1] This was done by assembling a small makeshift contraption on an editing table—two overlapping metal plates with windows the size of a single frame of the film are placed upright, with enough space between the plates to slide in the reel of film. Behind this window is a naked bulb lying on its side—it is turned on to light up the image that is then captured by a still photographer. In the absence of a film scanner, this remains the only method available to extract an image from a strip of celluloid at NFAI and I am not aware of any other book or author apart from Khopkar who has used it, though the apparatus likely ran through a few other hands.

As it turned out, the freelance photographer who was contacted by the department said that he no longer did the job and I was asked to wait for another photographer (who did not turn up) and finally instructions were given to have it done with an in-house camera. After initial hand-wringing over not finding a memory card, a cheerful young employee turned up with a DSLR camera, but as we found out in a couple of minutes, the camera came with a telephoto lens and was hopelessly inadequate for the task at hand. It did not help that the rusted metal window that was meant to help us take the photograph was not able to hold the frame firmly in place either. When the camera did have a go at the image (from a considerable distance, in almost no light), it was blurred and low resolution. A young man trained to work in film restoration suggested trying our phone cameras—we placed a sheet of white paper on the small circle of light built into the Steenbeck machine (to view film negatives), placed the film reel flat over it, braced two bobbins (the plastic circle around which celluloid is rolled) one atop another, perched my mobile phone on the bobbins to steady it and took a photograph of the film reel (about four frames in one image). I emailed the image to the publisher who confirmed that the resolution was good enough for publication—the smartphone whose intrusiveness I often complain about turned out to have a high definition resolution camera—and it is entirely thanks to the kindness and sincerity of that young technician that we gathered all the images we needed for this book, reel after reel, photograph after photograph, both of us pausing at several moments to take deep breaths at the sheer beauty and power of the cinematic shard in our hands.

It was precisely such passion and joy in cinema that had led to the establishment of NFAI and its catalogue in the first place. Shivendra Singh Dungarpur's documentary *Celluloid Man* chronicles the perseverance and foresight of the archivist P.K. Nair who set up NFAI in 1964.[2] It was entirely due to Nair's efforts that some rare and almost-destroyed footage was rescued. Film scholar Ashish Rajadhyaksha writes, 'India has had the poorest record of film survivals, with the National Film Archive of India possessing less than 5 per cent of everything that has been made.'[3] The earliest films have suffered the most. Nair claims to have acquired 10–12 of the over 1200 silent films made between 1912 and 1931[4] (records of these decades are so poor that every scholar has a different figure for the number of silent films made). Nair is credited with a photographic memory of the films he collected and the great lengths he went to acquire and restore reels from all over the country. However, the concrete reality of the archive we have at present is more akin to a mausoleum for film. In *Celluloid Man*, the noted film-maker Shyam Benegal succinctly diagnoses the two crucial components that go into a healthy archive: (a) individual(s) with vision and passion for curatorial work, (b) knowledge of what professional archiving involves at the administrative level.[5] My own observations attest that the system is woefully regressing in resources, process and vision. Current efforts seem nowhere close to stemming the bleed.

I am aware that this present narrative is entirely the representation of one researcher's experience—it cannot adequately represent all the many activities sustained by NFAI—and I am equally aware that laments about the slow disintegration of several archives in this country are also fairly predictable. Nonetheless, we cannot afford to indulge in self-congratulatory nostalgia for an influential black and white film heritage or its national repository when the films would be much better served if turned over to conservation specialists who have more accountability than the present system proffers. This would hopefully mean updates in technology, service and governance structures. I was told that NFAI at present is not equipped to work on preservation and restoration of master copies—these are outsourced through tenders—and only 550 films in its safekeeping have been digitised (this was done nearly a decade ago according to sources there and any further digitisation is again subject to government process). There are efforts to support research and publication with some annual grants (frugal by most standards) but the outputs of the majority of these projects are hagiographic and will not compare favourably with the best film scholarship in India or elsewhere. Somehow the understanding of archives has been mostly reduced to the running of air-conditioning in a vault, lining books in a library and the screening of films for festivals. In these conditions, the researcher is at risk of being a floating dispensable entity. This was certainly the feeling in my chest as I navigated the streets of Pune to locate a bored notary official to sign off on an indemnity bond (that familiar 500 rupee stamp paper) with our promise to use images ethically and give appropriate credit to NFAI along with a nominal fee for each image printed.

The mission was accomplished but not quite—the book manuscript that we thought was complete had to be extended to this reflective essay, not just as a metanarrative to research/writing but because we felt that our research has to speak beyond a temporary inhabitation of archive spaces, beyond analysis of cinematic text and technique and into a responsible consumption of works of art. The genesis of every archive starts with an impulse to save, to record—but one realises soon enough that the archive itself is a self-propelling narrative, an amorphous coming together of the fruition, slippages and quests of its record-keeping. In extension of this empathy with the archive, this book hopes to record the profound artistic nurture offered by the films of the era. These films deserve to endure for long and to be enjoyed by many more like us.

Endnotes

Introduction: The Promise of Black and White Cinema in Independent India

1 The two men that the director Guru Dutt decided to have with him on the crane were not actors but cinematographers he had worked with—V. Ratra, the man behind the camera, was the cinematographer for *Baazi* (Gamble, 1951) and V.K. Murthy, at the right edge of frame, was the cinematographer of three films studied in detail in this book (*Pyaasa*, *Kaagaz Ke Phool* and *Sahib Bibi Aur Ghulam*). He had worked as Ratra's assistant in the past. This is to indicate how Guru Dutt fully embraced the playfulness and possibilities of metanarrative.

2 B.D. Garg, *A Pictorial History of the Silent Cinema Era* (Noida: HarperCollins Publishers India, 2012), 16.

3 Ibid., 30.

4 Ibid., 52.

5 Ibid., 56.

6 Amrita Jain, 'Alam Ara Long Lost, was Never with NFAI: Founder-Director', *The Indian Express*, 17 March 2011. Available at: http://archive.indianexpress.com/news/alam-ara-long-lost-was-never-with-nfai-founderdirector/763632 (last accessed 2 May 2020).

7 Sumita S. Chakravarty, *National Identity in Indian Popular Cinema, 1947–1987* (Austin: University of Texas Press, 1993), 65–67.

8 Someswar Bhowmik, *Cinema and Censorship: The Politics of Control in India* (New Delhi: Orient BlackSwan, 2009), 123.

9 Ravi Vasudevan, *The Melodramatic Public: Film Form and Spectatorship in Indian Cinema* (New Delhi: Orient BlackSwan, 2015), 77.

10 Ibid., 45.

11 Rosie Thomas, *Bombay Before Bollywood: Film City Fantasies* (New Delhi: Orient BlackSwan, 2014), 4.

12 Priya Joshi, *Bollywood's India: A Public Fantasy* (Irvington: Columbia University Press, 2015), 2.

13 Ashish Rajadhyaksha, 'The "Bollywoodization" of the Indian Cinema: Cultural Nationalism in a Global Arena', *Inter-Asia Cultural Studies* 4, no. 1 (2003): 116.

14 Ravi Vasudevan, 'The Meanings of Bollywood', in *Beyond the Boundaries of Bollywood: The Many Forms of Hindi Cinema*, eds. Rachel Dwyer and Jerry Pinto (New Delhi: Oxford University Press, 2011), 17.

15 Bhowmik, 142.

16 Neepa Majumdar, *Wanted Cultured Ladies Only! Female Stardom And Cinema In India, 1930s–1950s* (New Delhi: Oxford University Press, 2010), 10.

17 Lalit Joshi, 'Cinema and Hindi Periodicals in Colonial India (1920–1947)', in *Narratives of Indian Cinema*, ed. Manju Jain (Delhi: Primus Books, 2009), 44.

18 Thomas, 106.

19 M. Madhava Prasad, *Ideology of the Hindi Film: A Historical Construction* (New Delhi: Oxford University Press, 2013), 24.

20 Vasudevan, *The Melodramatic Public*, 64.

21 Anil Saari, *Hindi Cinema: An Insider's View* (New Delhi: Oxford University Press, 2009), 7–9.

22 Majumdar, 10.

23 M.K. Raghavendra, *Seduced by the Familiar: Narration and Meaning in Indian Popular Cinema* (New Delhi: Oxford University Press, 2014), 17–18.

24 Nasreen Munni Kabir, *Guru Dutt: A Life in Cinema* (New Delhi: Oxford University Press, 2012), 1.

25 Rachel Dwyer, *Religion and Indian Cinema* (Oxon: Routledge, 2006).

26 Ruth Vanita, *Dancing with the Nation: Courtesans in Bombay Cinema* (New Delhi: Speaking Tiger Publishing Pvt. Ltd., 2017).

27 Sangita Gopal and Sujata Moorti, *Global Bollywood: Travels of Hindi Songs and Dance* (New Delhi: Orient BlackSwan, 2010), 45.

28 Rachel Dwyer and Divia Patel, *Cinema India: The Visual Culture of Hindi Film* (New Brunswick: Rutgers University Press, 2002) 10–11.

29 Richard Misek, *Chromatic Cinema: A History of Screen Color* (West Sussex: Wiley-Blackwell, 2010), 2.

30 Govind Nihalani, 'Through the Viewfinder', in *Encyclopaedia of Hindi Cinema*, eds. Gulzar, Govind Nihalani and Saibal Chatterjee (New Delhi: Encyclopaedia Britannica [India], 2003), 255–256.

31 Although, here it is worth taking a brief detour to acknowledge efforts of scholars like Ashish Rajadhyaskha and forums, such as Indiancine.ma and Shabistan (David Farris), in collating and notating many of the older texts.

32 Sathya Saran, *Ten Years with Guru Dutt: Abrar Alvi's Journey* (Gurgaon: Penguin Random House, 2008), 102.

Overture: Kamal Amrohi's *Mahal* (1949)

1 Majumdar, 189.

2 Vijay Mishra, *Bollywood Cinema: Temples of Desire* (New York: Routledge, 2002). Rachel Dwyer, 'Bombay Gothic: On the 60th anniversary of Kamal Amrohi's *Mahal*', in *Beyond the Boundaries of Bollywood: The Many Forms of Hindi Cinema*, eds. Rachel Dwyer and Jerry Pinto (New Delhi: Oxford University Press, 2011), 130–155. Meheli Sen, *Haunting Bollywood: Gender, Genre, and the Supernatural in Hindi Commercial Cinema* (Austin: University of Texas Press, 2017).

2 Bhowmik, 142.

3 Vasudevan, *A Melodramatic Public*, 10.

4 Dwyer, 'Bombay Gothic', 133.

5 Barbara Fuchs, *Romance* (New York: Routledge, 2004), 9.

6 Annette Insdorf, *Cinematic Overtures: How to Read Opening Scenes* (New York: Columbia University Press, 2017), 1.

7 Raghavendra, 108–109.

8 Dwyer, 'Bombay Gothic', 148.

9 Gerd Gemunden, *A Foreign Affair: Billy Wilder's American Films* (New York: Berghahn Books, 2008), 34.

10 S.V. Srinivas, *Megastar: Chiranjeevi and Telugu Cinema after N.T. Rama Rao* (New Delhi: Oxford University Press, 2009), 37.

11 Dwyer, 'Bombay Gothic', 139.

12 Ibid., 141.

13 The musicologist Ashok Damodar Ranade writes of the film music in the 1940s and credits Naushad with the moving film songs from a more spontaneous use of 'live' recording to the more technologically structured and controlled space of the studio. Ashok Da Ranade,

Hindi Film Song: Music Beyond Boundaries (New Delhi: Promilla & Co., Publishers, in association with Bibliophile South Asia, 2006).

14 Dwyer, 'Bombay Gothic', 143.

15 Fuchs, 130.

The Rebellious Image: Raj Kapoor's *Aag* (1948)

1 Dwyer, 'Bombay Gothic', 131; Joshi, 23.

2 Majumdar, 147.

3 Madhu Jain, *The Kapoors: The First Family of Indian Cinema* (New Delhi: Penguin India, 2009), 76–77.

4 Babak A. Ebrahimian, *The Cinematic Theater* (Lanham, Md.: Scarecrow Press, 2004), 42.

5 Jane Feuer, 'Spectators and Spectacles', in *The Film Cultures Reader,* ed. Graeme Turner (New York: Routledge, 2002), 240–241.

6 Richard Schechner, *Over Under and Around: Essays in Performance and Culture* (New York: Seagull Books, 2004), 29.

7 Annette Insdorf, *François Truffaut* (New York: Cambridge University Press, 1997), 26.

8 Constantin Stanislavski, *My Life in Art* (London: Bloomsbury, 2016), 47.

9 Chakravarty, 47.

10 Thomas, 260.

11 Majumdar, 153.

Female (Self) Portraiture in Monochrome: Nutan in Bimal Roy's *Sujata* (1959) and *Bandini* (1963)

1 Richard Schechner, *Over Under and Around: Essays in Performance and Culture* (New York: Seagull Books, 2004), 102.

2 Andre Bazin, *What is Cinema? Vol. 1* (Berkeley: University of California Press, 2005), 102.

3 Raghavendra, 184.

4 Gilles Deleuze, *Cinema 1: The Movement Image* (Minneapolis: University of Minnesota Press, 1997), 116.

5 Vasudevan, *The Melodramatic Public*, 153.

6 Naseeruddin Shah, *And Then One Day: A Memoir* (London: Hamish Hamilton, 2014), 49.

7 A rapid melodic vocal technique in raga singing.

8 Classic Legends - Nutan | S03 | Ep 10 - Full Episode | Javed Akhtar.' *YouTube*. Video File. 04 January 2015. https://www.youtube.com/watch?v=ZOjNCfFYhpI.

9 Chakravarty, 111–112.

10 Charles Chaplin, *My Autobiography* (London: Penguin Books, 1992), 152.

11 Ibid., 152.

Framing the Artist: Guru Dutt's *Pyaasa* (1957) and *Kaagaz ke Phool* (1959)

1 Jyotika Virdi, *The Cinematic Imagination: Indian Popular Films as Social History* (London: Rutgers University Press, 2003); Arun Khopkar, *Guru Dutt: A Tragedy in Three Acts* (New Delhi: Penguin India, 2012); Ravi Vasudevan, *The Melodramatic Public*; Raghavendra, *Seduced by the Familiar*.

2 Uma Rao, *Bisilu Kolu: Cinematographer V.K. Moorthy's Journey in Light and Shade* (Bangalore: Prism Books Pvt. Ltd., 2006); Chakravarty, 105; Kabir, 136.

3 Kabir, 117.

4 Ibid., 127; Gopal and Moorti, 23–24.

5 Sathya Saran, *Ten Years with Guru Dutt: Abrar Alvi's Journey* (New Delhi: Penguin India, 2011), 70.

6 Ibid., 102.

7 *Baazi* (1951), *Jaal* (1952), *Baaz* (1953), *Aar Paar* (1954), *Mr. & Mrs. '55* (1955), *Pyaasa*, *Sailaab* (1956), *Kaagaz Ke Phool* (1959).

8 Kabir, 159.

9 Deleuze, 12.

10 Ibid., 13.

11 Saran, 89.

12 Rao, 163.

13 V.K. Murthy, 'Interview' with Raqs Media Collective and C.K. Muralidharan in *Circuits of Cinema: A Symposium on Indian Cinema in the 1940s and 50s. June 2009.* Interview by transcript, December 1999. https://www.india-seminar.com/2009/598/598_interview.htm.

14 Ibid.

15 Khopkar, 32.

16 Vasudevan, 119.

17 Rao, 171–173.

18 Ibid., 143.

19 Ibid., 146. All translations from Uma Rao's *Bisilu Kolu* are the authors'.

20 Kabir, 128.

21 Rao, 146.

22 Kabir, 122.

23 Rao, 161–162.

24 Khopkar, 43.

25 Rao, 176.

26 Ibid., 216.

27 Ibid.

The Waiting Dissolve: Abrar Alvi's *Sahib Bibi aur Ghulam* (1962)

1 Francesca Orsini, 'Introduction', in *Love in South Asia: A Cultural History* (New Delhi: Cambridge University Press, 2019), 33.

2 Orsini; Ruth Vanita, *Dancing with the Nation: Courtesans in Bombay Cinema* (New Delhi: Speaking Tiger Publishing Pvt. Ltd., 2017); Lata Singh, *Raising the Curtain: Recasting Women Performers in India (Critical Thinking in South Asian History)* (New Delhi: Orient BlackSwan, 2017).

3 Kabir, 171.

4 Saran, 148.

5 Andrey Tarkovsky, *Sculpting in Time: The Great Russian Filmmaker Discusses His Art* (Austin: University of Texas Press, 2003), 38.

6 Saran, 144

7 Ibid., 144–145.

8 Ibid. 143.

9 Virdi, 137.

10 Rao, 206–207.

11 Saran, 147.

12 This turns up several times in the memories that Abrar Alvi's biographer records in *Ten Years with Guru Dutt: Abrar Alvi's Journey*. It is also discussed by Guru Dutt's biographer Nasreen Munni Kabir in *Guru Dutt*.

Conclusion: Fade to Colour

1 Nasreen Munni Kabir, *Conversations with Waheeda Rehman* (Gurgaon: Penguin Books, 2015), 86.
2 Ibid., 86.
3 Rachel Dwyer and Divia Patel, *Cinema India: The Visual Culture of Hindi Film* (New Brunswick: Rutgers University Press, 2002), 57.
4 Govind Nihalani and Saibal Chatterjee, 'Cinematography: Through the Viewfinder', in *Encyclopaedia of Hindi Cinema* (New Delhi: Encyclopaedia Britannica (India) Pvt. Ltd. and Popular Prakashan Pvt. Ltd., 2003), 255–256.
5 Dwyer and Patel, *Cinema India*, 59.
6 Vasudevan, *The Melodramatic Public*, 52.
7 Ibid., 86.
8 Nihalani and Chatterjee, 247.
9 Ramna Walia, 'Techno-Nostalgia: Colorization of K. Asif's Mughal-E-Azam', *Bioscope: South Asian Screen Studies* 4, no. 2 (2014), 147.
10 Ibid., 145.

Outro: Reel Number 13

1 Khopkar, xi–xii.
2 Shivendra Singh Dungarpur, dirs. *Celluloid Man*. Dungarpur Films, 2012. https://www.netflix.com/watch/80170612?source=35 (last accessed 30 January 2020).
3 Ashish Rajadhyaksha, *Indian Cinema: A Very Short Introduction* (New Delhi: Oxford University Press, 2016), 4.
4 Dungarpur.
5 Ibid.

Bibliography

Filmography

Aag (1948), directed by Raj Kapoor.
Aah (1953), directed by Raja Nawathe.
Aan (1952), directed by Mehboob Khan.
Andaz (1949), directed by Mehboob Khan.
Awaara (1951), directed by Raj Kapoor.
Baazi (1951), directed by Guru Dutt.
Bandini (1963), directed by Bimal Roy.
Barsaat (1949), directed by Raj Kapoor.
Celluloid Man (2012), directed by Shivendra Singh Dungarpur.
Citizen Kane (1941), directed by Orson Welles.
Devdas (1955), directed by Bimal Roy.
Do Ankhen Barah Haath (1957), directed by V. Shantaram.
Do Bigha Zamin (1953), directed by Bimal Roy.
Hum Hindustani (1960), directed by Ram Mukherjee.
Jagte Raho (1956), directed by Sombhu Maitra and Amit Maitra.
Junglee (1961), directed by Subodh Mukherjee.
Kaagaz ke Phool (1959), directed by Guru Dutt.
Madhumati (1958), directed by Bimal Roy.
Mahal (1949), directed by Kamal Amrohi.
Mother India (1957), directed by Mehboob Khan.
Mughal-e-Azam (1960), directed by K. Asif.
Pather Panchali (1955), directed by Satyajit Ray.
Pyaasa (1957), directed by Guru Dutt.
Sahib Bibi aur Ghulam (1962), directed by Abrar Alvi.
Seema (1955), directed by Amiya Chakravarty.
Shree 420 (1955), directed by Raj Kapoor.
Sujata (1959), directed by Bimal Roy.
Taxi Driver (1954), directed by Chetan Anand.

Bazin, Andre. *What is Cinema? Vol. 1.* Berkeley: University of California Press, 2005.

Bhowmik, Someswar. *Cinema and Censorship*. Hyderabad: Orient BlackSwan, 2009.

Chakravarty, Sumita S. *National Identity in Indian Popular Cinema, 1947-1987*. Austin: University of Texas Press, 1993.

Chaplin, Charles. *My Autobiography*. London: Penguin Books, 1992.

Classic Legends - Nutan | S03 | Ep 10 - Full Episode | Javed Akhtar.' *YouTube*. Video File. 4 January 2015. https://www.youtube.com/wabtch?v=ZOjNCfFYhpI (last accessed 4 June 2020).

Deleuze, Gilles. *Cinema 1: The Movement Image*. Minneapolis: University of Minnesota Press, 1997.

Dungarpur, Shivendra Singh. dirs. *Celluloid Man*. Dungarpur Films, 2012. https://www.netflix.com/watch/80170612?source=35 (last accessed 30 January 2020).

Dwyer, Rachel. *Religion and Indian Cinema*. Oxon: Routledge, 2006.

———. 'Bombay Gothic: 60 years of Mahal/The Mansion, dir. Kamal Amrohi, 1949'. In *Beyond the Boundaries of Bollywood: The Many Forms of Hindi Cinema*, 130–155. Rachel Dwyer and Jerry Pinto. New Delhi: Oxford University Press, 2011.

Dwyer, Rachel and Divia Patel, *Cinema India: The Visual Culture of Hindi Film*. New Brunswick: Rutgers University Press, 2002.

Ebrahimian, Babak A. *The Cinematic Theater*. Lanham, Md.: Scarecrow Press, 2004.

Feuer, Jane. 'Spectators And Spectacles'. In *The Film Cultures Reader*, 240–245. Graeme Turner. New York: Routledge, 2002.

Fuchs, Barbara. *Romance*. New York: Routledge, 2004.

Garg, B.D. *A Pictorial History of the Silent Cinema Era*. Noida: HarperCollins Publishers India, 2012.

Gemunden, Gerd. *A Foreign Affair: Billy Wilder's American Films*. New York: Berghahn Books, 2008.

Gopal, Sangita and Sujata Moorti. *Global Bollywood: Travels of Hindi Songs and Dance*. New Delhi: Orient BlackSwan, 2010.

Gulzar, Govind Nihalani and Saibal Chatterjee. *Encyclopaedia of Hindi Cinema*. New Delhi: Encyclopaedia Britannica (India), 2003.

Insdorf, Annette. *Cinematic Overtures: How to Read Opening Scenes*. New York: Columbia University Press, 2017.

———. *François Truffaut*. New York: Cambridge University Press, 1997.

Jain, Madhu. *The Kapoors: The First Family of Indian Cinema*. New Delhi: Penguin India, 2009.

Joshi, Priya. *Bollywood's India. A Public Fantasy*. Irvington: Columbia University Press, 2015.

Kabir, Nasreen Munni. *Conversations with Waheeda Rehman*. Gurgaon: Penguin Books, 2015.

———. *Guru Dutt: A Life in Cinema*. New Delhi: Oxford University Press, 2012.

Khopkar, Arun. *Guru Dutt: A Tragedy in Three Acts*. New Delhi: Penguin India, 2012.

Majumdar, Neepa. *Wanted Cultured Ladies Only! Female Stardom and Cinema in India, 1930s-1950s*. New Delhi: Oxford University Press, 2010.

Misek, Richard. *Chromatic Cinema: A History of Screen Color*. West Sussex: Wiley-Blackwell, 2010.

Mishra, Vijay. *Bollywood Cinema: Temples of Desire*. New York: Routledge, 2002.

Murthy, V.K. 'Interview' with Raqs Media Collective and C.K. Muralidharan in *Circuits of Cinema: A Symposium on Indian Cinema in the 1940s and 50s. June 2009.* Interview by transcript 1 December 1999. https://www.india-seminar.com/2009/598/598_interview.htm (last accessed 17 May 2020).

Orsini, Francesca. 'Introduction', in *Love in South Asia: A Cultural History*, 1–39. Francesca Orsini. New Delhi: Cambridge University Press, 2019.

Prasad, M. Madhava. *Ideology of the Hindi Film: A Historical Construction*. New Delhi: Oxford University Press, 2013.

Raghavendra, M.K. *Seduced by the Familiar: Narration and Meaning in Indian Popular Cinema*. New Delhi: Oxford University Press, 2014.

Rajadhyaksha, Ashish. *Indian Cinema: A Very Short Introduction*. New Delhi: Oxford University Press, 2016.

Rajadhyaksha, Ashish. 'The "Bollywoodization" of the Indian Cinema: Cultural Nationalism in a Global Arena'. *Inter-Asia Cultural Studies* 4, no. 1 (2003): 25–39.

Ranade, Ashok Da. *Hindi Film Song: Music beyond Boundaries*. New Delhi. Promilla & Co., Publishers in association with Bibliophile South Asia, 2006.

Rao, Uma. *Bisilu Kolu: Cinematographer V.K. Moorthy's Journey in Light and Shade*. Bangalore: Prism Books Pvt. Ltd., 2006.

Saari, Anil. *Indian Cinema: The Faces behind the Masks*. New Delhi: Oxford University Press, 2011.

Saran, Sathya. *Ten Years with Guru Dutt: Abrar Alvi's Journey*. New Delhi: Penguin India, 2011.

Schechner, Richard. *Over Under and Around: Essays in Performance and Culture*. New York: Seagull Books, 2004.

Sen, Meheli. *Haunting Bollywood: Gender, Genre, and the Supernatural in Hindi Commercial Cinema*. Austin: University of Texas Press, 2017.

Shah, Naseeruddin. *And Then One Day: A Memoir*. London: Hamish Hamilton, 2014.

Singh, Lata. *Raising the Curtain: Recasting Women Performers in India*. New Delhi: Orient BlackSwan, 2017.

Srinivas, S.V. *Megastar: Chiranjeevi and Telugu Cinema after N.T. Rama Rao*. New Delhi: Oxford University Press, 2009.

Stanislavski, Constantin. *My Life in Art*. London: Bloomsbury, 2016.

Tarkovsky, Andrey. *Sculpting in Time: The Great Russian Filmmaker Discusses his Art*. Austin: University of Texas Press, 2003.

Thomas, Rosie. *Bombay before Bollywood: Film City Fantasies*. New Delhi: Orient BlackSwan, 2014.

Vanita, Ruth. *Dancing with the Nation: Courtesans in Bombay Cinema*. New Delhi: Speaking Tiger Publishing Pvt. Ltd., 2017.

Vasudevan, Ravi. 'The Meanings of Bollywood'. In *Beyond the Boundaries of Bollywood: The Many Forms of Hindi Cinema*, 3–29. Rachel Dwyer and Jerry Pinto. New Delhi: Oxford University Press, 2011.

———. *The Melodramatic Public: Film Form and Spectatorship in Indian Cinema*. New Delhi: Orient BlackSwan, 2015.

Virdi, Jyotika. *The Cinematic Imagination: Indian Popular Films as Social History*. London: Rutgers University Press, 2003.

Walia, Ramna. 'Techno-Nostalgia: Colorization of K. Asif's Mughal-E-Azam', *Bioscope: South Asian Screen Studies* 4, no. 2 (2014): 137–158.

Index

About the Authors

Gayathri Prabhu is the author of *Vetaal and Vikram* (HarperCollins, 2019), *If I Had to Tell It Again* (HarperCollins, 2017), *The Untitled* (Fourth Estate, 2016), *Birdswim Fishfly* (Rupa Publications, 2006) and *Maya* (Indialog Publications, 2003). She has published in *The Journal of Commonwealth Literature*, *Routledge Handbook of Ecocriticism and Environmental Communication*, *Transnational Literature* and *Ecloga*. Her professional experience of over ten years in film and television includes assisting in direction and screenwriting. She is an Associate Professor at the Manipal Centre for Humanities, Manipal Academy of Higher Education (MAHE), Karnataka, India.

Nikhil Govind is the author of *Inlays of Subjectivity: Affect and Action in Modern Indian Literature* (Oxford University Press, 2019) and *Between Love and Freedom: The Revolutionary in the Hindi Novel* (Routledge, 2014). He has published in the areas of Indian aesthetic and political modernism and is on the editorial board of the *Indian Journal of Medical Ethics*. He is the Head of the Manipal Centre for Humanities, Manipal Academy of Higher Education (MAHE), Karnataka, India.

Click/scan this QR to view scenes described in the book.